MW01595383

More Mornings with the Dads

Sharing the Never-Ending Road of Grief
No Parent Should Ever Have to Take

Copyright © 2016 by Mornings With The Dads Inc. Individual authors hold the copyright to their respective work within this book.

Mornings With The Dads Inc., is a 501(c)(3) corporation registered in the State of Indiana.

Cover and interior design by Jerry Bennett of Bennett Books.

Cover illustrations:
Grieving Man © iStock
Coffee Cups © iStock

All rights reserved. No part of this book may be reproduced or transmitted in any form or by any means whatsoever, including photocopying, recording or by any information storage and retrieval system, without written permission from Mornings With The Dads Inc., the publisher and/or author.

Colophon
Body text is set in Times New Roman
Running heads, folios and Chapter headings set in Palatino Linotype.

ISBN-13   978-0-9825151-3-6
ISBN-10   0-9825151-3-8

Publisher: Bennett Books, A Publishing Resource for Independent Authors, (317) 902-7254

Printed in U.S.A.

All paper is acid free and meets all ANSI standards for archival quality

1

Dedicated to all grieving fathers
You are not alone.

And their beloved children
You are not forgotten.

CONTENTS

CONTENTS — Continued

Foreword

In 2009 I was asked to write a foreword to a book written by fourteen men who are coping with an indescribable tragedy … the loss of a child. I was approached because I could feel their pain. I had lost a son in 2005.

The book was *Tuesday Mornings with the Dads*, and included the story of two young brothers who never had a chance to see their Colts win the Super Bowl. The Saturday night before the game, Jake and Travis Findley were riding in an SUV that was hit by a train—killing both of them. When I returned to Indy following the game, I was contacted by Travis' third grade teacher, who told me the third graders in his class were having problems with the fact that their classmate was no longer there. When I went to the class, we talked about death, but more about life. That is when I met Chuck—Travis and Jake's father. That was the beginning of a special friendship with Chuck and, by extension, a kinship with all the Dads.

It is an honor to write the foreword for the second book. *More Mornings with the Dads* tells the story of seventeen additional men who share a common bond—the loss of children. These stories contain losses of children by murder, drugs, accident, illness and suicide. The stories are gut-wrenching. It also contains four follow-up stories from the original book. These updates give an insight on how time does not heal all wounds.

The men come together weekly to support, help and comfort each other and any and all fathers who need understanding. Men and women grieve differently. These dads have walked the walk and talked the talk of unthinkable grief in an era of real men don't cry. Their motto ... We get it.

I know if you read this book you will take some great lessons with you. We can learn a lot from the experiences of these men. We will learn how not to take the gift of children for granted. We'll learn that God is always in our lives, even in the worst of circumstances. And most importantly, we'll learn that, as important as it is to reach out to help others who are hurting, it is just as necessary to allow others to reach into our lives when we are experiencing pain. We will learn that no matter what the obstacles, no matter what the pain, and no matter how long it lasts, with God's help—and with each other—we can persevere through anything life throws at us.

Tony Dungy

Our Story Continues

This is the second in a series of books that should never have to be written: stories written by fathers about the tragic loss of their children—and the strength, hope and support they receive over a cup of coffee with fellow dads who "Get It." This volume includes seventeen chapters by dads who are new to our group, plus four follow–up chapters from dads whose stories appeared in our first book, *Tuesday Mornings with the Dads: Stories by Fathers Who Have Lost a Son or a Daughter.*

The purpose of the book is to give all dads who have lost children a bit of comfort by letting them know they are not alone. Our stories acknowledge the differences between moms and dads who are grieving. They also address the overwhelming reality that the loss of a child is so much more impactful than any other loss. We give our stories in our words, from our hearts. We have talked the talk and walked the walk. That is why "We Get It."

This was a tough book to write. As each dad wrote his chapter, he was compelled to relive the joys he had shared with his child, the hopes he had held for the child's successes … and the sudden loss of that child. But there is something therapeutic in the writing process, that I believe has helped in the healing process. You will note that the time periods of the stories vary from losses that happened in just this past year or so, to losses that occurred well over a decade ago. That is a living testament to the fact that time does not heal all wounds.

A special deep-hearted thanks goes to our editor, Dianne Martin. She is the editor of both books. These chapters are stories of children lost mostly by violence, accident or drugs. It takes a very special person to read and edit this topic. Through her empathy, sympathy and warmth she is able to sincerely feel our pain. It is apparent in every story.

This book is written by dads for dads. I would be remiss if I didn't mention the mothers and their contributions. They also have a group—the Southside Moms Group—that comes together for the understanding, healing and support. Their group is important to ours in a special way, as many dads have joined after seeing the comfort their spouses received being a part of the mothers group. There is more information about both groups at the back of this book.

It has taken seventeen months to complete this book. Early on, I started the venture of writing a chapter telling the story of my oldest son, Steve. As I was writing Steve's story, I lost a second child, my only daughter, Katie. But I realized the need to go forward and continue their stories. During this time, we have also had two dads awaiting the trials of those responsible for their children's deaths. These dads are related by marriage: one's son and the other's daughter were married—and both were lost in a tragic arson-explosion in Indianapolis. They have had to witness the loss of their children being played in the media for months, *years*, as they endure the crawl of the criminal justice system. Thanks to their devotion to this project, their stories appear for all to read.

I believe they, and all involved, agree with me: if this book helps one dad, the challenge of writing it was worth it.

Henry Pawlik

A Note from the Editor

When I was invited to write a note here, I welcomed it as an opportunity to pay homage to the men who contributed chapters for this book. The "Dads." Capitalized throughout, to denote members of the group. I hope to convey the high esteem I have for them—and how humbled I have been by this project, as a writer and as a parent.

I know what it is to write about a painful, intensely personal event. And there is nothing more devastating than the loss of one's child. I know these Dads had to persevere through anguish and tears. Yet, each story is offered with profound tenderness, grace, raw candor and disarming humility. Unassuming, unexpected, poetry. How does one write when he cannot see the words? How does he go on, when each attempt submerges him in a swell of grief? I believe the force that pushes him onward, through the heartbreak, is *love*. A deep infinite love for the child he is honoring—and a compassionate merciful love for an unknown dad somewhere "out there" who is experiencing the same excruciating pain. Each story is both a tribute and a gift. An offering for the sake of helping someone else. I do believe that writing serves the writer, and is an invaluable tool for exploring emotions and taking a step toward healing. My own primary purpose was to help guide these men through this process while providing an editorial safety net. But each could have written—and kept it for himself. Or he could have avoided, or omitted, the tougher revelations. The fact that each is willing to share his story—the one that permeates his thought day and night—and publish it, as is, vulnerabilities and all, is an act of pure selfless generosity.

This project has been a blessing to me, as well, most significantly in that it has helped me be a better parent to my son, Jack. I do not take even a second of my time with him for granted. I don't sweat the small stuff—I relish it. And no matter what, each time we part ways, we give each other a kiss and say, "I love you." Thank you, Jack, for this. And to the Dads, for these greater life lessons.

My thanks to Jerry Toomer for introducing me to the original Dads group, which meets on Tuesdays; for drawing me into these book projects that have enriched my life and elevated my priorities; and for being a steadfast friend and colleague. My thanks, also, to Henry Pawlik, the fearless leader of the more recently formed Thursday group. He established Mornings with the Dads as an official not-for-profit organization, initiated this second book, and led the Thursday group through the process. My sincere thanks to him for welcoming my participation and for inviting my insight along the way. My immense appreciation to the Thursday Dads for stepping up and accomplishing this undertaking with enthusiasm and commitment. And to the Tuesday Dads and out-of-town Dads who also contributed stories and so graciously supported this endeavor on all levels. A special thank you to the Moms, too. I admire and respect you, and cannot begin to fathom your strength.

I treasure the interaction I've had with each of you, and it's been a pleasure getting to know you and your children. I believe your stories will, literally, help *save* other grieving dads.

With much love and gratitude to all of you.

Dianne Martin

OUR STORIES

THE DADS GROUP

Lindsay Ann Allen
May 14, 1985 – December 14, 2003

In late July, 1992, my oldest sister, Mary Jo, died. She was forty-eight years old and had battled cancer bravely for over a year. As we were walking out of the funeral home to head to the cemetery, my dad was walking behind my wife, Tracey, and me. I heard him say, tearfully, "No parent should bury their child." I heard him, yet it didn't resonate at that moment what he was experiencing.

My mom had died twenty-two years earlier, and had also battled cancer; she was only forty-seven years old, and was leaving behind our dad and six children. I was thirteen, and the youngest. Mary Jo, nearly fourteen years older than I, had taken me under her wings and assumed the role of mother for me until our dad remarried a few years later.

In 1997, five years after Mary Jo passed, my dad died. My other sister, Sissy, had already been diagnosed with breast cancer and passed away in 2001. As with Mary Jo, she, too, was forty-eight years old when she died.

After Sissy's passing, our family slowly made its way back to a normal life. Eventually, it seemed like we were even finding some joy again, as our kids were busy with school, work, and activities, and my wife and I got back to our own busy schedules.

Fast forward two years to early December, 2003. Our family loved Christmastime and we had already done some decorating and shopping. The holiday was a bit tough for me, because my mother had died on December 9 and my dad on December 21. I did my best not to seem sad around the kids.

On Thursday, December 11, my daughter Lindsay, who was eighteen years old, wanted to go to lunch. She and I had been going to breakfast or lunch regularly for a couple of months. This time, she began talking about going to the Indianapolis Colts game on Sunday. She had never gone, but her boyfriend's family had tickets and had invited her to go with them. She told me they had an additional extra ticket, and asked me to go, too, but I declined so I could relax at home and watch the game on TV. Lindsay continued talking about her future and the goals she was making. I was excited and beaming with pride as she talked away. She noticed me smiling and said, "What are you thinking?" I replied, "I am so proud of you." Then she was silent, and I was surprised to see tears well up in her eyes. In short order my eyes began to well up, too. It was a special moment for me, to know how much that meant to her. As we were leaving, we made plans to meet again for lunch the following Monday, December 15.

On Saturday, December 13, I worked at my office till noon. On my way home, I heard on the radio that Saddam Hussein had been captured. When I arrived at the house, I immediately turned the TV on. Lindsay walked in, sat down next to me and said, "What's going on?" I told her about Hussein's capture and she said, "Cool!"

She asked if she could borrow my Colts jersey to wear to the game and I said yes. She then asked me again to go with them to the game, and I again declined. She sat with me a few more seconds, then off she went. On her way to the kitchen, she noticed a spray can of snow and promptly wrote MERRY CHRISTMAS—in large lettering, like that—on the patio doors. When she was done she peeked over, with a mischievous grin, to see if I had noticed. I shook my head and grinned. A bit later, carrying the Colts jersey, she was leaving. As always, I got a hug and an "I love you." When she walked out the door, I did not know that would be the last time I would ever see her.

The following day was Sunday—game day—and she was off with her boyfriend, Nick, to meet at his parents' house. She called and talked to Tracey before they headed to the game. Tracey said Lindsay was so excited and had said to tell me she loved me.

The game began at 1:00 p.m. My brother Bob and my brother-in-law Tim came over to watch the game. Tracey and our fourteen-year-old daughter, Katelin, headed out for some holiday shopping. As I watched the game, I thought I might have a remote chance of seeing Lindsay in the crowd, but never did. The game ended around 4:00 p.m., so I expected her around 4:30. Tracey and Katelin got home at about that time and Tracey began preparing dinner for all of us, including Lindsay and Nick. Katelin was busy wrapping gifts to put under the tree. Five o'clock came and went and no word yet from Lindsay. Even as six o'clock approached we wondered where she was, but didn't feel alarmed.

A few minutes after 6:00 p.m., Tracey shouted from the other room that two police cars were pulling into our driveway. The distress in her voice was obvious. I hesitated, as I couldn't imagine why the police would be stopping at our house. I made my way to the front door with Tracey. Katelin was standing off to the side. I opened the door as one of the officers was about to step up onto our porch. I could see the distress in his face. I looked toward the driveway and saw a second officer walking toward us. He hadn't realized we had opened the door, and he quickly tried to place something behind a shrub. But it was too late. I had seen what it was. A pink purse. It was Lindsay's purse. At that moment, I knew why they were at our home.

The officers entered our home and we headed to our family room as I anticipated the words about to be spoken. The officer explained to Tracey, Katelin, Bob, Tim, and me that Lindsay had been in an auto accident and hadn't survived. There was a silence … followed by wails and sobbing. In an instant, we had gone from the anticipation of Lindsay arriving and sharing how much fun she had had—to the reality of never seeing her again.

As one officer retrieved Lindsay's purse from the shrub, the other officer explained what information he had. He did not know where Lindsay had been taken, but gave us a business card with a number to call for more information.

My son, Kyle, who was twenty-one, was not home. Once we collected ourselves, Tracey made a couple of calls and located him. Kyle's friend drove him home, and Kyle joined us as we huddled in our grief. As we consoled each other, we began to realize we needed to make more calls.

My first call was to Dorothy, my stepmom. She had always referred to herself as our second mom and we all loved it. Dorothy had lost her oldest son, Chuck, in an auto accident in the early sixties. Both she and my dad had lost a child, and now Tracey and I were sharing the pain of losing a child. I did not know how to tell her the news that her granddaughter had died. I knew she would be devastated; yet her faith was so strong, I knew she would give me some comfort. I was not wrong. As soon as I heard her voice I lost my composure, and she knew something bad had happened.

Most of the family who lived nearby came to our home that night. As the night went on, it increasingly seemed impossible that Lindsay was gone. All I wanted to do was be with Lindsay, but I knew I had to be home for Tracey, Kyle and Katelin. We all would break down over and over as we tried to figure out what, next, to do. A deep fog consumed me as I tried to process what had occurred. I recall walking into the kitchen and seeing my brother-in-law Tim leaning against the cabinets. We looked at each other and I saw the sadness in his face, the tears. He shouted out to me, "*Steve!*" It tore my heart out. I went to him and we hugged and cried together. As I started to leave the kitchen, there it was. MERRY CHRISTMAS on the patio doors. My heart sank deeper. We left that reminder on the patio doors for many months, until it wore off.

The next day the details of the accident were starting to become clearer. Lindsay's boyfriend, Nick, who had been driving, and whom Lindsay had been dating for almost two years, had slid off a curve on a road near our home. As his Jeep slid off the road on that sleety gloomy day, it struck a tree on the passenger side, where Lindsay was sitting.

13

Lindsay died instantly. As I was watching the postgame for the Colts victory, and prepared to watch the second game, my daughter's life had slipped away less than a mile from our home.

My brother Bob allowed his big brother instincts to take over, as he had done so many times over the years. He saved us in so many ways. He consoled us, made calls, and helped us figure out the next step and the next. He gave Tracey and me a tremendous gift by helping us those first few days and, truly, that has never stopped. He drove us to our church to speak to Father Vincent. He took us to the funeral home to help us with the arrangements. ... As Tracey and I made these decisions, we were told that Lindsay's head injuries were severe and that they recommended a closed casket. We were devastated. We wanted to see Lindsay. As the tears flowed we agreed to remember her as she was.

Our home soon filled with our families and friends. Kyle's friends and Katelin's friends all came to support them. Lindsay's friends came. We were overwhelmed by the kindness. I recall walking from one room to the next, each one full of family and friends. I remember the chatter, the tears, and even a smile as stories of Lindsay began to flourish. I remember posterboards of pictures being constructed by Kyle, Katelin and their friends. I would disappear on occasion and sob uncontrollably. Then I would return to all the love in our home. Tracey and I would catch each other's gaze from across the room as we each tried to talk to as many as possible. As I watched her, I could see the intense sadness in her eyes. It broke my heart. I was not sure how we could possibly survive this crushing heartache.

Lindsay's favorite color was pink, so we got pink ribbon, and Katelin and many others cut the ribbon so we all could wear a piece for the wake and funeral Mass. It was indeed a beautiful sea of pink.

As we prepared for the funeral I was so mindful of the outpouring of love from our families. Tracey is the oldest of seven siblings. Her family represents the best any person could marry into. My father-in-law, Lloyd, and mother-in-law, Charlotte, are two of the kindest and most loving people I know. Their example of faith, family and love is reflected in each of their children. Each member of Tracey's family gave so much to help each of us. My own family gave so much, too. I was the youngest of six children, surrounded by my amazing three surviving siblings, Mark, Bob and Greg; my equally amazing stepmom, Dorothy; and my terrific stepbrothers, Larry, Gary and Jim Nolan, who had always treated me as their little brother. Both Tracey's and my families have always been there for us. I wish I could name each one, but they all know how much we love them.

Since both of our families were so large, we anticipated quite a few people to attend Lindsay's viewing. We arrived at the funeral home early. I can't and won't describe the heartache to see her closed casket for the first time. Earlier that day, I had left the house and gone to the department store to find a gift for Lindsay. I knew I would know when I saw it. I went to the jewelry department, and it didn't take long when I saw a beautiful pink cross. I bought it and, walking out to my car, I began to sob, trying to hide the enormity of my pain. I sat in the parking lot for awhile simply crying. When I found a moment, I left and went home. I went up to my office at home and wrote Lindsay a note, which said, *I am so sorry I did not keep you safe. I will love you forever. Daddy.* I put the note in the small jewelry box, with the cross, and wrapped it in Christmas paper and ribbon. After the family spent time with Lindsay at the funeral home, I placed the wrapped box on her casket. It was later placed inside her casket and buried with her. I just wanted her to have this gift for Christmas.

It wasn't long before we began seeing family and friends for her viewing. It began at 4:00 p.m. Tracey, Kyle, Katelin and I, and a beautiful picture of Lindsay, stood by her casket and received what seemed to be an endless line of people. Lindsay was a loving, compassionate, funny person. She adored her brother and sister. She was a protector for so many and passionate in helping her family and friends. The ripple effect of her loss was vast. We cried, we hugged, and we smiled as beautiful stories were told about her. I had no idea how many lives she had touched in her short life. Sometimes a person's inner beauty can be exposed by the simplest gesture. As one story after another was shared, I noticed a heavyset young man in line by himself. It was finally his turn and I could see how uneasy he was, but he bravely walked up to me and, looking me in the eyes, said, "Mr. Allen, I really didn't know Lindsay, but when she saw me at school she always said hello and asked me how I was." He went on to say that nobody really talked to him, but that she always had, and that it had meant the world to him. My eyes, already red and swollen, welled up again with tears. He finally said, "I thought you should know that about your daughter." We all knew Lindsay was a remarkable young woman, but as this night went on we were humbled and so very proud of her. It was a profound blessing to have such an outpouring of love.

The next day was Lindsay's funeral Mass and burial. It was a day much like the day of her accident ... cold, sleety, snowy and gloomy. Since my first experience with losing a loved one, and all those after, this had become the day I hated. I did not want to endure one more day of a burial. As much as I prayed and begged not to let my little girl go, God had a different plan. A plan I could not understand, and still don't understand.

Losing a child, then planning a funeral and enduring that process, was only the beginning of the grueling challenges that were about to consume our lives. I remember those first few days after Lindsay died, the world just kept going. I thought to myself, "Don't they know what I'm feeling...?" The pain.... The ache inside me kept growing, but I couldn't shout it out like I wanted.

A week after Lindsay died, I felt compelled to start journaling. I was fearful I would forget details that I was sure would be important to me years later. So I began writing about the last couple months of my interaction with Lindsay and the family. Within a few days I was at the last few days of her life.

Following the funeral, the void in our lives seemed to widen with time. We understood our families and friends, all those who grieved for Lindsay, had to move on with their lives just as I had when my parents and sisters passed. But, for me, this grief was different. I fought hard to hide my sadness every single day. Tracey and I both were still consumed with a crushing pain inside. We would go out for Sunday breakfast or lunch, or dinner on occasion, and find ourselves talking about Lindsay, then crying, and then trying to hide the tears from those nearby. This went on for several years.

I realized early this would be the biggest challenge of my life. Losing Lindsay had plunged me into a level of grief both unfamiliar and unimaginable, and created an emotional catastrophe in my life. It was an emotional cancer that I wasn't sure I could survive. I knew part of me had died the day Lindsay died. I also knew that, because of my struggles,

Kyle and Katelin were being deprived of the best dad they should have. Tracey and I melted together with this pain, and then a few years passed and we struggled as a couple. We fought hard to survive this massive burden of grief.

And then, in 2006, my brother Greg died, at the age of fifty-four. He was buried December 1, 2006. Another long illness, another December funeral.

I've had a life of loved ones battling terminal illness. Endless hospital-stays and doctor-visits. It's been brutal to watch these illnesses slowly take the lives of those I love. I loved each one and hated becoming so familiar with the grieving process. I did not want to lose them, yet knew it would be merciful if their suffering would end. Each time, I grieved ... but survived. But, even after my brother's death, I was still trying to survive losing Lindsay. Because there is no mercy in the sudden loss of a child. No end of suffering. Life stops, tragically. And the world keeps going.

I had continued to journal throughout these years, sensing that documenting my thoughts might help me heal. Several years later I realized my writing had become a necessary part of each day; but even so, it was not helping me heal as quickly as I wanted.

In 2011, Tracey heard of a dads group that got together once a week. She told me I needed to go. In 2012, I slowly got the courage to—and it was the turning point I needed.

This group of men showed me that I wasn't alone or crazy. It is incredible, the similarities of our grief and the challenges we face after losing a child, whether regarding work, family, or faith ... and, of course, pain. I believe that each Dad who is sharing his story in this book could write an entire book of his lost child (or children) and the journey of that loss. However, I believe the compilation of the Dads' stories, in one book, is a more powerful offering. Each Dad has unique experiences in his loss—and yet you, the reader, will see how much we have in common, too, through our grief. If you are a parent who has lost a child, and you read the collective journey, you will recognize at least some of the shared elements. You will realize you are not alone. You will realize you are not crazy.

Eleven years after losing Lindsay, I still feel the pain. I have come a long way, but the truth is, that pain will never go away. Yes, time helps, as does the support of others. My healing comes not from the support of one single person, but from the support of many: the Dads group; my incredible friends, like my best friend, Dennis Greene, who hung in there with me through the dark days; my brothers and stepbrothers; my in-laws; and my beloved second mom, Dorothy, whom I lost this past year.

My wife, Tracey, has been with me for every single loss in my life except my mother. She has taken my hand with each loss and given me exactly what I've needed, to endure. Even as she endures the loss of Lindsay, today, she continues to courageously drag me kicking and screaming forward. Always forward. I doubt words could ever express my love for her. The truth is, I could not have survived *this* loss without Tracey and my children.

Today, Tracey and I are blessed to have three grandchildren—Blake, Kingsten, and Raylen—who give us great joy. To our son, Kyle, and daughter, Katelin, thank you for your unconditional love through this difficult journey. You, too, give us immense joy. And I am positive Lindsay will join us in saying how proud we are of you both.

About a week after Lindsay died, I was sitting in my office at home and noticed a piece of scrap paper with some writing on it. I was stunned to see it was from Lindsay. It simply read, *Daddy, hope your having a great day! Love Linz.* Her note is framed and hanging on my wall at work. It's a cherished gift to read that every day.

More recently I received another surprise gift. Soon after Lindsay's death, we placed a cross at the accident site. It is a dangerous curve—the cross has been destroyed by other accidents that have occurred at the same place. Usually by the next day, I have a new cross, with her picture on it, back up. The cross, I hope, reminds others to slow down. On November 9, 2014, I made a new cross and replaced her picture and flowers. After cleaning the area, I walked back to my car. I have to park about a hundred yards away, in the lot of a city park. I was carrying Lindsay's old cross, old flowers, and parts from a car that had wrecked there a few weeks earlier. As I reached our vehicle, where my wife was waiting for me, I noticed a red car pull into the park and stop. A lady got out and approached me. She said, "So you're the 'Cross Keeper.'" She reached out to me and hugged me. She said that, as her children became old enough to drive, she had them drive by the "cross," to show them how important it is to be careful driving and how fragile life is. She extended her sympathy to my wife and me, and thanked us.

We were stunned and tearful. Tracey and I see this as a sign that, even in death, Lindsay's beautiful heart continues to shine for us and strangers.

We all strive to make such an enormous loss evolve into something positive, but we have to fight for it, because the pain is persistent and the challenges are many. Men are taught to be strong—be the tough one—but losing a child can affect all aspects of your life.

I am profoundly humbled by this opportunity to share Lindsay's story. I hope those of you who have lost a child will recognize your own story among these, and find some answers to your broken heart. I hope you can see you are not alone.

If you're overwhelmed, reach out. There is no shame in asking for a little help. I regret it took me so long. Our Mornings with the Dads is a group of exceptional men. We are and will be brothers forever!

Linz, I will love you forever,
Daddy

Steve Allen

Adam Brown
July 17, 1982 – August 6, 2008

Adam is the youngest of our three children. He was adventurous, energetic, and loved life. Hardworking and honest in all his efforts. His friends told us that if they ever needed anything, he was always willing to help. There was not a better friend.

In the fall of 2000, Adam moved to Colorado to attend Colorado Mountain College in Leadville. He could lie on his bed in his dorm room and see the two highest peaks in Colorado—Mt. Massive and Mt. Elbert—both over 14,000 feet. In Colorado, because of the cold weather, many people have two seasonal jobs. In the summer of 2002, Adam moved to Frisco, where he worked for a landscape company in the warm months; and in the winter he worked in the warehouse at Copper Mountain, a ski resort. At the landscape company he was the irrigation manager, taking care of homes for seasonal residents. He loved his jobs and living in Colorado.

In the fall of 2006, he moved to Wilmington, North Carolina, so he could work with an irrigation company and be employed year-round; but after working a two-week pay period, he went into the office to pick up payroll for those who had worked with him, and was instructed to tell them they would be paid the following week. He told the owner the men had worked hard and needed their pay. The owner again refused to pay them. Adam insisted, and finally the owner relented. Adam asked for his check as well, and stated he would not be back.

Adam loved music. He had an enormous collection of Phish, Yonder Mountain, Grateful Dead and Dave Matthews Band CDs. He and his friends drove to Red Rocks to see groups, as well as to Boulder and Denver. It was nothing for him to travel to see bands on long weekends or holidays. In 2007, Adam traveled back to Colorado from North Carolina with his mother. She had an atlas and wanted to check off the states he had been in. He said it would be easier to tell her the ones he had not been in—because there were only two. We have no idea what those two states could be, and his friends could not tell us either. We went to Hawaii on spring break in 1994, so we know he had been there, as well.

Adam played golf as much as he could, but the golf season in the mountains is very short. On Wednesday, August 6, 2008, he took part of the day off to play at the Copper Mountain golf course. He and others had set up the game the night before and needed a fourth. A guy who also worked at Copper Mountain had called Adam on several occasions wanting to play golf with him, so they decided to see if he could play. He said he could. They met at the course, played a round of golf, and had dinner in the dining room. Following dinner, this fourth player, who worked at the marina and had after-hours access to the boats, suggested he and Adam go on a boat ride on Lake Dillon. They agreed to meet at the marina, and when Adam went home to change clothes, he asked his roommates if they wanted to go on the boat ride, too. Fortunately one of them decided to take the opportunity since he was leaving the next day to return to school. It was this friend who was able to tell us later what had happened.

The person they were meeting, who had arranged for the boat, had had several beers before getting on the boat. They traveled across the lake, which is several miles, and stopped at another bar across the way, where they had another beer. Adam's friend told us that, at one point during their outing, Adam was leaning against the windshield of the boat, saying he was the luckiest man in the world, being able to see the beautiful sunset over the Rockies—and that he named all of the mountain peaks that surround the lake, marveling at God's beauty. As they were returning across the lake, and were a couple hundred yards from shore, the driver decided to do a doughnut. Adam and his friend were standing at the front of the boat and Adam nearly fell out, but his friend was able to grab him. The driver did another doughnut and this time Adam was thrown out of the boat. The water in the lake is runoff from the snow and is fifty degrees. They searched the area where Adam had gone in, but couldn't see him. They went back to the marina and called the Summit County Sheriff's Office. This was about 9:00 p.m.

Our nightmare began about 3:00 a.m. on Thursday morning, when we received a call from this friend who had been on the boat with Adam. He told us there had been an accident on the lake, and that they could not find Adam. He and Adam's other roommates were searching the banks in hope he had swum to shore.

My wife, Debbie, and I packed our bags, crying and praying that everything would be okay. My sister came over and made flight reservations for us, and my brother came to do what he could. We were out of the house and waiting at the Indianapolis airport for our flight at 7:00 a.m. Debbie had called our other two children, Abigail, in Houston, and Nathan, in Myrtle Beach. While waiting for our flight, I called a pastor friend whom we had become very close with, and gave him the news. I asked for him and the others in his church to be praying. He assured me they would.

We arrived at the Denver airport and were walking briskly to the car rental when Debbie's phone rang. It was a good friend of Adam's. She had heard the news and was distraught. She told us she would not be able to be with us, because she was getting married that weekend and was at the airport to pick up family. We got our rental car and headed up I-70 toward the mountains and Frisco. We were in such shock and disbelief. It was a quiet ride up the mountains. We rounded the curve outside Silverthorne and saw Lake Dillon. It looked so calm and peaceful. It was difficult to imagine it was holding such tragedy.

We arrived at Lake Dillon and went immediately to the marina, where we saw several police cars and a boat trailer. We walked to the end of one of the docks and sat down. After our eyes focused we could see, through the bright sunlight, the sheriff's boat and many men around it. We suspected this was the area they were searching for

Adam. We sat there for what seemed like an eternity. People would come by and ask if we knew what was going on, and we would have to relay the story through our tears.

The sheriff arrived, and he was such a comforting and calming influence for us. He assured us they were doing all they could but were having difficulty locating Adam. The driver of the boat and Adam's friend were having difficulty pinpointing the location. The sheriff said they had searched the shoreline of the lake the night before—but had to call it off after several hours. They resumed in the morning and also had avalanche dogs in the boats. The dogs could detect human scent in the water better than in the snow. He assured us they would stay until they located Adam. He also told us they believed it was no longer a rescue but a recovery. He or another officer stayed with us the remainder of the day. He also informed us the driver of the boat had been arrested the night before for boating under the influence, but was released in the morning, after making bail.

We stayed on the dock the entire day, watching as they searched for Adam's body about two hundred yards away. A lady from Wisconsin, who was there on vacation, talked with us and asked if she could organize a prayer vigil. We told her we would appreciate it. Adam's roommates came to the lake and met us. They were very upset. They were upset with the acquaintance who had bugged Adam to play golf (the driver of the boat), and they were upset with themselves. They felt in some way responsible, but we assured them there was nothing they could have done. We were just glad that one of his roommates had gone along. We didn't know the driver, and if there hadn't been a third person —a witness—the driver might have come to shore and not reported it. He might have claimed later that he had dropped Adam off and left. Then we may have never found Adam. We were also thankful Adam's friends had come to us at the lake, because we did not want to leave. They were so thoughtful and got us whatever we needed, such as jackets and food.

Adam's boss from Copper Mountain arrived at the lake, too, and told us how much he had enjoyed working with Adam and how good an employee he was. He asked if we had accommodations and said we could stay at the condos at Copper Mountain—which was only a few miles from the lake and would give us solitude. He stayed at the lake for several hours with us and offered to do all he could. We thanked him for his kindness and told him we would see him in the evening.

There was another spectacular sunset over the mountains as the lady visiting from Wisconsin came to set up for the prayer vigil. Many of Adam's friends and coworkers came to be with us. I was flabbergasted that the driver of the boat came to the vigil. He introduced himself to me, and I just did not have much to say to him. As we made a circle on the dock and lit candles to sing "Amazing Grace," we could see the men working in the distance, trying to find Adam. Not long after the vigil, the dive team came back in. They were stopping for the night.

The sheriff told us they were not having any luck locating Adam with the equipment they had available. They had asked Colorado State Parks if they could use its side-scan sonar. They use it to inspect dams in the lakes in Colorado, and for this kind of an event as well. The sheriff said they were hopeful but had not heard back yet. He also told us the lake has many deep spots that are as much as 350 feet deep. The divers can dive to only seventy-five feet because of the elevation and added pressure. If they did locate Adam, they might not be able to bring his body up—if it was too deep.

The next morning we returned to the lake. The head of Colorado State Parks had arrived with the side-scan sonar, and the team was already on the lake searching for Adam. The sheriff said they arrived early and immediately got into the water. He also said the area where they were searching would not be visible to us from where we'd been sitting. They wanted to move us to the other side of the lake, and to a less conspicuous place. It was a campground, and they had cordoned off an area for us and their command post. There were many officers around throughout the day, and they were so helpful and kind to us. Adam's employer at the landscape company arrived with the man Adam had worked for as the irrigation manager. They were shocked and so upset about the accident. They stayed with us several hours and said so many nice things about Adam and how much they loved working with him. They talked about his humor and his compassion for others. A Fox News truck showed up, and the sheriff went to talk with them. He came back and said they wanted to interview us—and that we could do it if we wanted, but that we didn't need to feel like we must. We agreed to do the interview, and the sheriff went back to them and set up the rules. He stayed with us during the interview, and I am sure he would have called a halt to it if it had got out of hand. He was so protective of us throughout the entire process. The first question the reporter asked was, "Being a pastor, what does this do to your faith?" I answered her that it strengthens my faith and that I do not question my Lord. I do not remember anything else about the interview except that Debbie did a great job handling the situation.

That afternoon we received word from the sheriff that they had located Adam's body, and that he was in forty-seven feet of water. They had hopes of getting him up soon. The day wore on without success. We heard the divers had gotten him part of the way up, but then lost him back down. Adam was six feet three inches tall and weighed about 180, so he was a big guy to pull up from forty-seven feet. The sheriff also told us the divers were getting weary. At the altitude of 9,000 feet, and the depth of forty-seven feet, they could be down for only a short period of time—and had to be checked each time by medical staff before going back in. This was the only high-elevation dive team west of the Rockies, and it was a volunteer group. What an incredible group of men we will be forever indebted to.

The coroner arrived as night fell on the lake. She told us she would be on the boat when Adam was recovered, to do a positive ID. It had begun to rain, so Debbie and I sat in her car while it rained, and she asked us questions about Adam and whether he had any distinguishing marks. The only thing we could remember was, a few years earlier, Adam had been at a party and had placed his hand in a doorjamb. Somebody, not knowing he had his hand there, closed the door and crushed his finger. Adam lost the tip of his left middle finger. The coroner said that that would be enough information, along with other identifying features we had mentioned.

By this time, the divers were bringing the boat in and were stopping for the night.

Saturday morning came, and when we arrived at the lake the dive team was already out. A storm had come through and they were concerned the buoy and the basket marking the spot of Adam's body had moved overnight. They were relieved to find it all still intact and in position. The sheriff continued to keep us informed throughout the day. There were many attempts to recover Adam, but because of various issues, they had failed. The sheriff came to us late in the day and asked if we wanted to ride out to the spot where Adam's body was. We said yes. When we got to the spot, it was difficult to think Adam was just forty-seven feet away, in that cold, dark water. The dive team was going to have to stop diving for the day, because they were putting their health in jeopardy. But as we were returning to shore, the divers passed us on their boat, going back out to try one more time. When we got to shore, we looked back. The sun was behind some clouds, but a sunbeam was shining on the spot where Adam was. Debbie commented that they would get him up this time. We waited several minutes, then the command center erupted in activity. The sheriff came to us and said they had Adam in the boat. It was both a sense of relief and unabashed grief and sadness. We watched as the boat sped to shore and the sheriff's department descended on the dock to help take him off the boat and place him on a gurney. He was in a blue rubberized water-recovery bag. The department surrounded him as they brought him to us. As we approached they left us alone. We could feel his body through the bag. Adam was literally frozen. His left arm was up and bent, with his hand behind his head. The divers told us that this positioning had been very helpful, because it had given them somewhere to grab hold of him. Debbie continued to touch him all over, and I went to thank the divers. We were so thankful they had put their lives on the line for Adam.

On Sunday morning we went to church with the man Adam had worked for at the landscape company and his wife. The sermon was "Trust and Obey" from Proverbs 3:5-6. That afternoon we started making plans for a memorial service in Colorado and arranging flights for Abigail and Nathan. Copper Mountain gave us a banquet room overlooking the golf course, and the landscape company provided the decorations. We set the service for Tuesday, August 12.

Monday morning we met with the sheriff. He had spoken with the district attorney, and they were considering charging the driver with vehicular homicide. A boat is not considered a vehicle, according to the statute, but they thought it would be worth the effort. After meeting with him, we left for the airport to pick up Abigail and Nathan. They were, of course, very upset and full of questions. We drove to the lake and discussed what we needed to do. The coroner had contacted us and said that Adam's condition was such that we could not transport him to Indiana. Our only choices were to have him buried in Colorado or have him cremated. We chose to have him cremated. Abigail and Nathan were a stabilizing influence on both Debbie and me. It was so good to have them with us. Adam's friends and roommates surrounded all of us those many days, and we are so grateful to them.

On Tuesday we made final plans for the memorial service and for our return flight to Indiana on Wednesday. The sheriff had informed us they were going to charge the driver with criminally negligent homicide. When we arrived at the memorial service many of Adam's friends were already there. The sheriff and many others from the department were there, too, as well as the dive team. We invited people to write stories about Adam, and we had many people tell stories. It was an evening of remembrance, support and love for Adam. Debbie spoke eloquently about our son, and Abigail and Nathan spoke about their "little brother." I spoke, as well. Adam had a good friend in Leadville who had two Labradoodles, Bonita and Luna. Adam would sometimes take one of the dogs with him on a trip. They attended the service, too.

On Wednesday morning we picked up Adam's ashes and went to Red Rocks, where we scattered some of his ashes in an undisclosed location before returning to Indiana. Upon our arrival at the Indianapolis airport, we were met by good friends who had brought a van big enough for all of us. When we got home we were surrounded by family, friends and neighbors, all wanting to know what they could do. Debbie, Abigail and my sister, Jane, started planning a memorial service for Sunday at Brown County State Park. The next few days were a blur to me. I had a wedding to perform at the state park on Saturday, of a couple from out of state, that I had agreed to months before. I was able to get through the wedding—and the couple stayed overnight, to come to the memorial service.

The memorial service at Brown County State Park was attended by hundreds of friends. We were also visited by a red-tailed hawk. Debbie's brother, Mike, had noticed it was sitting in a tree, watching the activity. When we made a circle that was probably forty yards across, the hawk flew down into the circle and around the circle and back up into the tree. We heard many great stories as we laughed and cried. We all spoke once again and thanked everyone for being a part of Adam's life.

The next day we left to drive to Colorado to get Adam's things and his car. We had heard from the sheriff that the driver had been arrested and charged, so we also met with the assistant district attorney while we were there. He explained the charges to us, and the procedure. He felt they had a strong case for vehicular homicide.

We were back in Colorado the following week for a preliminary hearing on the charges. The ADA told us they were going to change the charges to BUI and criminally negligent homicide. We were in Colorado every two weeks, until the trial, for hearings. As we got closer to the trial date in January, the defense attorney wanted to reach a plea deal. The ADA suggested we look at it, because in liberal Colorado, and as a well-known defendant, he could walk in a jury trial. At the last opportunity, we agreed to allow him to plead guilty to BUI and no contest to criminally negligent homicide. The sentencing hearing took place in February, and Abigail and Nathan flew in to speak in court. Debbie and I spoke, as well, through our tears. The judge sentenced the driver to two years in state custody and five years probation. We were in Colorado seventeen times in twenty-two months, advocating for Adam and speaking on his behalf as they attempted to release the defendant early. The driver served less than four months in prison and a little more than a year in a halfway house.

Beyond making the many trips to Colorado to represent Adam, Debbie and I also began looking for special ways to remember him.

We were so indebted to the sheriff of Summit County, and the dive team, that we asked what we could do to make their job easier. We agreed to work at purchasing a side-scan sonar for the department. They would own it and provide the expertise in its use, but it could be shared with other counties in Colorado. In 2010, with the help of family and friends, we gave them $42,000 to purchase this equipment.

We also hold an annual memorial golf outing to raise funds for various projects that Adam would have supported. We have contributed to Purple Heart Alpacas—a friend of Adam's, who has suffered from PTSD since serving in Iraq, raises Alpacas for therapy for veterans. Columbus Youth Hockey receives a check each year to install new dasher boards. Both of our sons played hockey from age five in the

Columbus Youth Hockey program. They competed at the highest levels in youth hockey, and both played high school hockey for the Columbus Icemen. In 2009 the hockey board began presenting the Adam Brown Award to a senior hockey player who exemplifies the ideals that Adam displayed. We grant a scholarship each year for the recipient of the award. We also send an annual donation to the Summit County Sheriff's Office to purchase new equipment for the water rescue team.

Debbie and I are so blessed to honor Adam in these ways. We now live our lives as Adam once wrote: "I cannot imagine one day without a cause, or not trying to brighten another person's day."

Greg Brown

Leslie Christine Cook Dickerson
April 1, 1978 – April 26, 2003

Our oldest of three children, Leslie lived an active childhood that greatly involved her participation in softball and basketball. In her earlier years of playing softball, her Grandpa Cook would pay her a dollar for every home run she'd hit. I think, if I remember right, one summer she hit about thirteen! Her first introduction to sports was on a tee-ball team that was all boys except for Leslie and one other girl. That team was the Cubs. With me being a lifetime Dodgers fan, Leslie said the Dodgers would always be her #2 team, next to the Cubs. I never could change that order.

Leslie continued with her softball-playing up through her high school days and even after her first year of college. She got to play on Center Grove High School's softball team her freshman and sophomore years and wound up completing an undefeated pitching record as the team's #2 pitcher. During her last season of playing on our Center Grove Lassie League team (the Dodgers!), she wound up badly spraining both ankles when sliding into home plate during our first game of the summer season. She was then sidelined until our last game of the season. One of my greatest memories is bringing her into that last game and her getting to pitch the last inning. It was hard for me to hold back my emotions, seeing her strike out that last batter … and knowing this was the end of her softball-playing career. I had the great pleasure of coaching girls fast-pitch softball for sixteen years in the Center Grove Lassie League and travel teams for both our daughters.

Being in the Center Grove High School marching band—the Center Grove Marching Trojans—brought wonderful memories, too. All of those contests culminated with Center Grove winning the 1995 Bands of America Grand National Championship at the Hoosier Dome in downtown Indianapolis. This contest consisted of over ninety high school marching bands from all over the country.

Leslie graduated from Center Grove High School in 1996 and went on to college at Indiana University in Bloomington. She graduated with her four-year bachelor's degree in applied health science with an emphasis in nutrition science. During high school and in college, she worked part-time at our local Boston Market restaurant to earn some spending cash. While she worked at Boston Market, she would meet her future husband, John Dickerson, who worked as a shift manager. They fell in love and were married on October 27, 2001.

In 2002 my wife, Linda, and I purchased a condo as an investment property and offered it to Leslie and John as a place where they could live. At that time, Leslie had gone back to school, enrolling in the dental hygiene program at Indiana University-Purdue University Indianapolis (IUPUI) in Indianapolis. They were living in a small studio apartment with their two cats and were really cramped for room. They jumped at the chance to take possession of our condo. Life was really going well for all of us.

On the morning of Saturday, April 26, 2003, Linda and a friend of hers helped deliver some storage cabinets to Leslie and John's condo to help them out with the organization of their belongings. Between work and school, Leslie was still in bed on that morning. When leaving, Linda felt compelled to go back upstairs and sit on the side of Leslie's bed and talk a bit longer. Linda said later that she had felt an "inner voice" telling her not to leave.

Much, much later that day, our lives would change forever. Leslie and John both had to go to work that day at their Boston Market restaurants—Leslie on Indy's east side; John on Indy's north side. At some point around 3:00 a.m. or so (early morning, Sunday, April 27), our phone rang. It was John calling, wondering if Leslie had come to our house after her work shift ended (our other daughter, Leanne, was at our home visiting from Chicago, where she was going to college at the time, so he was hoping maybe Leslie had stopped by). I told John that Leslie was not here. He then told me there had been some trouble on Friday night at Leslie's restaurant when a man who worked there made some advances toward her, resulting in an incident. Linda and I had not heard about this incident from the night before. John said he would drive out to the restaurant on the east side. I got dressed and drove out there, also, looking every inch of the way for a sighting of Leslie's car. When I got to the restaurant, John was already there, as were several law enforcement officers. It was then that I heard more about the seriousness of the incident that had occurred on Friday night.

More and more police arrived. I, along with John's parents, drove around the area looking for Leslie. Fear was really settling in by now. Pretty soon the Indianapolis Fire Department arrived with a search team and search dogs. We called local hospitals to see if Leslie had been taken to one of them. I went home and brought my wife out to the restaurant, too. It was such a helpless feeling. I/we looked over an area a mile or two each way from the restaurant. Heck, I even opened the dumpster at the restaurant and took a peek in there. Time seemed to be at a standstill. We searched, and waited, through daylight and the morning hours. Later, in the afternoon, the police told us we should probably go on home and they would let us know when news of Leslie's whereabouts was found.

When we arrived back at our home, quite a crowd had gathered there. We all felt so hopeless. We were told that news of Leslie's disappearance had been announced at our church that morning, and that many people had fallen to their knees praying for our daughter's safety.

Early that evening the TV was on in our family room, and the local news was coming on at 6:00. Then came those words we will never forget … "Late breaking news … the body of a female has been found on the east side of Indianapolis at the Boston Market restaurant." We all collapsed in shock. I will *never* forget my wife's chilling wailing cry as those words were heard. At that moment, our phone rang. It was the police department, trying to get ahold of John. They had to call him first since he was Leslie's husband, and were having trouble getting ahold of him, so they called our home phone.

Shock quickly gave way to anger ... "How could this have happened?"

We were later told that our beloved daughter Leslie had been stabbed twenty-six times by her coworker, her body wrapped up and placed in the bottom of the dumpster at the restaurant, then covered with trash to obscure her. It was the same dumpster I had opened and looked inside. It is by the grace of God that I did not find her there. Her assailant then drove her car a few blocks away and left it there after robbing her, too.

The police reviewed the restaurant cameras and knew exactly what had happened. It was all on the restaurant's surveillance tapes. We were told Leslie put up a powerful struggle in fighting for her life. The police went to the man's apartment on the east side of Indy and apprehended him while he was trying to escape. He was so demented he had taken the knife he killed her with and placed it in his kitchen butcher's block at his home. The man was married and had a small child. We later heard there had already been two warrants issued for his arrest (DWI and public intoxication), and that he was working illegally in the U.S. Why hadn't he been apprehended before???

How do we prepare for the funeral of our twenty-five-year-old perfectly healthy daughter? Much of this time period is a time blur. But, with the help of so, so many people, we got through it. From our family's initial excruciatingly painful private viewing, to the placing of her body at the cemetery, is a period of time that is too tough to recall. The showing at

41

Greenwood Christian Church started in the afternoon and went until after 11:00 p.m. that evening. There were so many people. The hallway of the church had so much memorabilia of Leslie.... I don't recall where it all came from and who helped prepare all of this. The funeral home people were wonderful to us. We hugged and cried all night, it seemed. I don't think I ever sat down. No words Linda and I could come up with would ease the pain and suffering felt by Leslie's sister, Leanne (age twenty), and brother, Devin (age eighteen). And I remember, in a blur, folks coming through the receiving line that evening ... many of Linda's schoolteaching friends, Leanne's school friends, Devin's Center Grove High School basketball team and coaches, Leslie's first-year dental hygiene class at IUPUI, our church friends, my work friends, and countless others. We had family in from all over the country.

Our minister, Shan Rutherford, presided over the funeral. Shan had baptized Leslie, was the minister at her wedding, and was now handling the difficult task of burying her. The tremendous outpouring of love from family, friends, and so many other people was something we will never forget. The funeral procession was so long that, as we were arriving at Forest Lawn cemetery, cars were still in line leaving the church (a few miles away).

After the funeral, we had to mentally prepare to be thrust into the court system for the next eighteen months. As a family, we sat down with the Marion County prosecutor and his team, and were told what to expect and what kind of options we had. I remember the first time we went to court and got to see the man who had taken our daughter's life in such a vicious manner. As a line of prisoners, all chained together, was coming down the hallway, I asked our lawyer if Leslie's murderer was among them, and was told he was. He was pointed out to me. As he shuffled by, chained to the other prisoners, it was only by God's power that I refrained from attacking him. Again, I can't describe my emotions at that time. Each month, we were called to court for a pre-trial hearing. Many of these court appearances left us feeling so frustrated and helpless. In our minds we kept saying, "How could this have happened?" Usually, when we left court, TV station and newspaper reporters were there, wanting interviews.

Finally, on November 3, 2004, the judge sentenced Leslie's murderer to seventy-five years in prison. This sentence, we were told, was probably the best we could hope for, if we could hope for anything. On that day, before a packed courtroom, three of us spoke from the witness stand. I went first, as Leslie's father. Then John, her husband. And finally, another member of our family, who spoke fluent Spanish and said things to this man—I have no idea what they even were. What a time of emotions! We also felt much sorrow for the murderer's family, who were also in the courtroom.

Life goes on, as the saying goes.

I buried my mother in 1995 and my father in 1998, after they had lived long productive lives. My wife has survived two bouts with breast cancer, in 1998 and 2000. The second bout was life-threatening. I lost my job at the telephone company in 1999, after thirty years of service, due to corporate downsizing.

But, how does one "go on" after losing a twenty-five-year-old healthy daughter? I can't provide an adequate answer. I've had many moments, asking God, "Why did this happen?"

I know, keep the faith.

We got to have Leslie in our presence for twenty-five years and twenty-six days. Actually, Linda got to have her about nine months longer, but kept her within before the grand entrance. Again, what wonderful memories we have of her. From the moment we told both sets of our parents at dinner one evening that Linda was expecting our first child, little did we realize what joys welcoming a child into the world would bring. So many of these memories have been captured by pictures, slides, tapes, certificates, trophies, ribbons, cards, articles of clothing, plus everything else I'm leaving out while trying to write this. These memories we will always cherish. How can we say goodbye to someone we loved so much and who brought so much love, care, and affection to all of those she touched? I guess we have to realize what we had here on this earth was a twenty-five-year, twenty-six-day loan and the note-holder is our heavenly Father. And, He told us that this loan is now paid in full. Leslie is now up in her heavenly home with our parents and so many, many others who have touched her life and ours. She's constantly telling us not to worry and be sad because, for her, she's now experiencing the "time of her everlasting life"—and, just wait and see what's in store for us in the future. Thank you for these brief moments in time with us here, Leslie. We can't wait to see you again. While we're still here on earth, we'll try to do you proud. You've been such a blessing to us. To you, our love forever.

My involvement with the Thursday Mornings with the Dads group began while reading the newspaper one day. On Wednesday, September 2, 2009, I was looking at our local paper, the *Daily Journal*, and I saw a picture of a man I had worked with at Indiana Bell Telephone Company. In fact,

Jim Nathan and I were in the same carpool for a number of years. Jim's son had been killed by a drunk driver in 2001, and Jim was now part of a support group of fathers who had lost children in just about any form of death one can imagine. Reading this story touched me so that I had to call Jim and become part of this group. I came the next day. I sat in my vehicle early in the morning on September 3, 2009, waiting until I saw Jim pull into the parking lot of the Bob Evans restaurant where the breakfasts were held at that time. As it turned out, another new father showed up that same day, so there were two of us attending our first Dads meeting. The warmth of this group of men who had each lost a child was something I was needing. Listening as each Dad told his story ... my heart ached for every one of these guys. The saying of our total group (Tuesdays and Thursdays) is that, "We're all a part of a group no one wants to be part of ... but we're so happy a group of this type is out there for those of us who need it." Jim's words, as quoted in the *Daily Journal*, are so true for all of us: "Nothing is private. It gives you a chance to go ahead, speak your feelings, and everybody else lets you know, 'I've done it. I'm there with you.'" Reading the book *Tuesday Mornings with the Dads* was quite an agonizing experience for me. It took me a while just to get through the preface, the foreword written by Tony Dungy, and the "Our Group Begins" section written by Adolf Hansen. Then, after finally getting through all of this, what followed were fourteen gut-wrenching stories written by fathers grieving for the losses of their children. I think it wound up taking me three days or so to just make it through the book the first time I read it. I kept thinking, fourteen dads, and fifteen children lost. And then I thought about all the other dads out there with their losses. It's overwhelming!

After reading Tony Dungy's book *Quiet Strength*, I thought it would be a neat idea if somehow I could get the Coach to autograph it. My wife and I had met Coach Dungy and his wife at the Indianapolis Symphony shortly after the Colts had won Super Bowl XLI. Not too long after that, I sent a note to the Colts office with my request. Nothing happened for quite awhile after I mailed my letter. I guess I didn't think he would really do it. One night, I got home from work and checked our home voicemail. To my *shock* and *surprise*, there was a voicemail from Coach Dungy, saying he would be pleased to sign the book, and where I should mail the book to. When the book came back to me, these words were written inside the front cover: "To Dave & Linda, God can level out even the very rockiest paths. Keep your eyes on Him and let Him guide you! Tony Dungy" and "Rom. 8:28."

Each year, since Leslie's death, Linda and I award a graduating senior from Center Grove High School a $1,000 scholarship. By doing this, we try and keep Leslie's memory fresh in our minds and the community. We are part of the Center Grove Scholarship Foundation. We award the scholarship on Senior Awards Day to a student who plans to pursue a health care studies program at a four-year college. We were able to start doing this in 2003. It's always a tough day, getting up in front of the auditorium full of people and speaking, but I always say a little prayer before I speak, asking God to help me get through this. And of course, Linda is right there with me.

How can we help others? By being part of the Dads group, and being there for others when they need us. One of the main reasons we're put on this earth is to care for people. There are, of course, all kinds of ways to do this. By what's happened to each of our Dads and their families, we have to be there for each other. A kind word, a shoulder to cry on and, in our cases, having a cup of coffee together each Thursday morning.

As our group has grown, many of our wives have begun meeting together in a "Moms" version of our Dads group. It's so important for them to reach out to other mothers with losses, just like we Dads reach out. We're all in this together. Once in a while the Moms group will invite us Dads to join them, and we get to buy them dinner!!

As a group we continue to look for good out of tragedy. I know, at times it's hard to think that way ... nearly impossible. But if we all keep looking, maybe, just maybe, there's more good out there for all of us to find. My good friend Chuck Findley wrote the following words in the group's first book, which I feel so accurately echo my (possibly all our Dads') beliefs:

- Never take a single day for granted, NOT EVER.
- Live your life to the fullest and be the best person you can be in the process.
- Parents, love your kids with all your soul and make sure they know you love them.
- Believe that the only hope we have after our time on earth is to trust God, and that we will see our loved ones once again in heaven.

When, as a group, we began discussing writing this book, I thought, sure, I can do that. But, as time went on, I was to find out how tough it really was for me to sit down and put pen to paper and really do this! It would make me relive the whole experience of going through Leslie's death, and I thought, can I really do this? As I wrote my chapter, by hand ... literally pen to paper ... my thoughts took me back through those twenty-five years and twenty-six days when I was blessed to have Leslie here with me. I cherish all the good memories. There are things I did, especially when coaching Leslie in softball, that I wish I hadn't. Why was I so hard on her sometimes over a ballgame? For those times, Leslie, I am truly sorry. But, the good times so outweigh the not so good ones. I love you and sure do miss you. These thoughts are also echoed by the rest of your family. And, now you are an aunt to two little girls—Kayleigh Christine and Aria Brynn—and a baby nephew, Declan Bryce, who was born November 24, 2014.

In closing, a common question we all get from time to time, and especially when meeting people for the first time, is, "How many children do you have?" My answer, and it's an easy one: "We have three. One in heaven and two with us here on earth."

David Cook

Nicolas William Habicht

June 11, 1983 – May 23, 2004

The reservations had been made. Our family was looking forward to going to Las Vegas to celebrate our son Nic's twenty-first birthday on June 11, 2004. My wife, Mary Lou; our daughter, Malia; son-in-law, Kurt; Nic; and I were all making plans to go. We would arrive in Las Vegas a few hours before midnight the day Nic would turn twenty-one. We thought there would be nothing stopping us from going and celebrating Nic's birthday, but we were so wrong. We never made it to Las Vegas.

Nic had just completed his sophomore year at IU Bloomington, where he had been living in his fraternity, Sigma Pi. He had decided to change majors and wanted to stay in Bloomington to attend summer school. The fraternity closed for the summer, so Nic had made arrangements to sublease a room in a house where a group of high school friends from Center Grove had been living all year. Nic was going to stay in the room of his friend Jimmy, while Jimmy was doing an internship in Texas. They had known each other since elementary school, and Jimmy had accompanied us on many spring break vacations while they were in middle and high school. They were like brothers. Mary Lou and Malia had tried to persuade Nic to come home for the summer, and not go to summer school, but Nic was looking forward to living in Bloomington during the summertime. He had secured a job at Abercrombie and had signed up to take summer courses. He moved out of his fraternity and into the house on May 12. We never had a chance to visit him in the house.

On Friday, May 21, Nic came home and spent the day having fun by our pool with his friend Abby. That night we tried to talk him into staying home and going out to dinner with us, but he was anxious to get back to Bloomington and was looking forward to starting his new job the next day. As he was driving out of the driveway, little did I know that would be the last time I would ever see him leave our home. The next day our lives changed forever. We would never be the family we once were.

In the early morning hours of Saturday, May 22, 2004, a fire broke out on the first floor of the house that Nic had just moved into. There were four boys in the house that night. Around 8:30 in the morning, while I was at Home Depot, my wife got a phone call from Jimmy's mom, Nancy, asking her if she knew where Nic was. Mary Lou told her that Nic was at the house in Bloomington. Nancy then said she had heard there had been a fire at the house. My wife was relieved to hear that it was a fire and not a car accident—thinking, *these boys are young ... they could get out of a fire.* Nevertheless, she immediately called me to tell me, and I got home as quickly as I could. We called Malia and told her we were heading to Bloomington because of the fire. My wife kept calling Nic's cell phone, praying he would answer it, but he never did. She called Nancy again to get Jimmy's phone number so that we could get in touch with the landlord. Nancy told her Jimmy could not talk on the phone, because he was too upset—they had heard that Joseph had died in the house fire. Joseph was another Center Grove graduate who had been living in the rented house. We had known him since Nic was young. Joseph was raised by a single mom, and we remembered seeing them sitting together in church. Our hearts ached for Joseph's mom. We did not know how she could survive losing her only child.

Still heading towards Bloomington, we called Bloomington Hospital to see if Nic was there, and they said he wasn't. We then somehow got a call from Methodist Hospital in Indianapolis, and they said Nic had been Lifelined to Methodist and that he was gravely ill. We got to Methodist as quickly as we could. We called our daughter and she and her husband arrived at Methodist before we did. When we walked into the emergency room, we were met by Malia and Kurt. The nurses quickly took us to the room where Nic was. It was terrible seeing him lying there. He was covered with black soot and smelled of soot. They had him hooked up to machines. The day before, he had been swimming at our pool with his friend—and now our family had been thrown into a nightmare. I asked the doctor if Nic was going to make it and he said no. My wife said God performs miracles every day. The doctor said that Nic had been taken first to Bloomington Hospital, where the doctors had worked on him for over an hour to get his heart beating again, and was then Lifelined to Methodist. The doctor at Methodist said they were moving him to ICU.

During the fire, Nic had made a 911 call to summon help. His call saved the life of one of the boys who had been staying at the house the night of the fire, and who was already unconscious from the carbon monoxide.

Since they were not keeping Nic in the ER, we took this as a good sign that maybe there was hope. We thought that God would not take him away from us. We needed Nic—how could we go on without him?

By the time he was moved to the intensive care unit, Nic's friends, and our friends and family, had started arriving at the hospital. This was in 2004, before social media was in common use, but the word spread quickly about the fire. The waiting room in the ICU was so crowded they moved us to another room. I remember coming out of the ICU doors to a sea of people lining the hallways, all there for Nic. Many of his friends were crying. They would go into the ICU two or three at a time to see Nic. It was unimaginable that this was really happening.

My wife and I, our daughter and son-in-law, and some good friends spent the night at the hospital. There was no change in Nic. Our minister had been there earlier in the day and had had to leave to go be with Joseph's mom to help her in this terrible crisis. My wife and friends went to the chapel to pray. That was all we could do … pray for a miracle.

The next morning, the doctor and nurses were suggesting we remove Nic from life support. My wife wanted a brain scan done, first, to make sure there was no brain function. Since it was a Sunday, we had to wait for an X-ray technician to come in and perform it ... and it was confirmed that there was no brain function. We all surrounded Nic's bed while the nurse slowly turned off Nic's oxygen machine, and he immediately passed away. It was 1:45 p.m. on Sunday, May 23, 2004. It was too hard to believe that this was really happening. As we walked out of the ICU for the last time, we could not believe that we were leaving our son. He should be going home with us. We were mentally and physically exhausted. It was just too overwhelming, what was happening in our lives.

Three boys died ... Nic, Joseph, and another friend, Jacob. It was unimaginable ... something you read about in the newspaper, and you feel sorry, but you know that it would never happen to your family.

The next day, we had to go to the funeral home to make plans to bury our son. We had never been through this before. Friends helped in the ways they could, including bringing meals to us. Neighbors brought us meals, too—an effort initiated and coordinated by a neighbor who had contacted other neighbors. Our daughter, Malia, is a first grade teacher, and some of her students and their families live in our neighborhood and brought us meals, as well. We were so grateful for this support from friends, neighbors, and Malia's class. Family from out of town had started coming in, too.

Our life seemed like a blur at this point. We were just going through the motions of what needed to be done. We felt an outpouring of love from so many people. Somehow we made it through the showing the night before the funeral. There were so many of Nic's high school friends and college friends who attended his showing and funeral. I felt sorry for

Nic's friends. They had never lost someone their age before, and they took it very hard. Many of Malia's first grade students and their parents attended, too.

Nic's funeral was on a Thursday, and the following Monday I decided to go back to work, as did my wife. We felt it was best to try to get back to normal, as much as we could, although normal for us would never be the same. We both went to the cemetery every day. Sometimes I would stop by and have lunch at the cemetery. We had driven by Forest Lawn so many times before this happened, never imagining we would be going there to visit our son. It was and still is so hard to believe that he is gone. We ask for signs from Nic, and we both believe we get them. People will say that he is in a better place, but we want him here with us, and we wish heaven could have waited for him. He was so full of life and always had a positive attitude, and we are certain he would have had a successful future. He loved little children, and we know he would have been married with children of his own.

In the years since Nic's passing, we have found a few ways to help us cope, but we carry this pain with us every day.

In 2005, with the help of some amazing friends, we began the Friends Forever Memorial Golf Classic—an annual memorial golf tournament in remembrance of Nic and his two friends who also died in the fire, Joseph Alexander and Jacob Surface. The golf outing is held in August, and friends of Nic, Joseph and Jake come from all over the country. We have over two hundred golfers each year. It is a very emotional day for our family. Funds raised from the event are used for high school scholarships that my wife and I present to three graduates from Nic, Joseph and Jacob's high school. We also donate funds to fire departments, food banks, Christmas Angels and other local charities. Proceeds are also used to provide smoke and carbon monoxide detectors to individuals in need. It was because of the carbon monoxide poisoning that the boys perished.

In 2009, at the urging of my wife, I started attending the Dads group. We all understand the sadness and hurting that we constantly have. When we meet, sometimes we laugh and sometimes we cry, but we are surrounded by men who understand what we're going through.

In 2010, Mary Lou started a Moms group for moms in our area who have lost a child—a group of moms who have compassion and empathy for each other. They all have the same broken heart that they have to learn to live with.

This past May, 2015, it has been eleven years since we lost Nic, and we still want to see him walk through our door. Nic was a wonderful son and brother, and a friend to many people. There is a huge void in our lives without him. It is still impossible to believe that this has happened to our family. We try to go on, but there is a constant void. Weddings of his friends are hard. Learning what his friends have achieved as adults is hard, too. But losing a child is something we have to learn to live with. Some days are good, and other days we just do our best to get through it. We miss him every day. We cry silent tears. We still go to the cemetery, but not as often.

Since losing Nic, we have been blessed with two beautiful grandchildren—Mallory Grace, who is eight, and Chace Nicolas, who is five. Nic is buried in the Garden of Grace, so Mallory has Grace for her middle name. Chace Nicolas is named after his Uncle Nic. Chace resembles Nic, and he is such a sweet and loving little boy, like Nic was. They know all about their Uncle Nic and, for them, going to the cemetery is as normal as going to McDonald's. We have picnics at the cemetery, and we talk about Uncle Nic all the time. They have taught us that we can be happy again.

Mary Lou and I still have not made it to Las Vegas. It doesn't seem right to go there without Nic. Everything in our lives, we compare to before Nic died and after he died. Nic was our beautiful treasure. He will remain in our hearts forever, and our heartache will never fade.

The following quotation from Elisabeth Kübler-Ross and David Kessler's book *On Grief and Grieving* is so true:

The reality is that you will grieve forever. You will not "get over" the loss of a loved one; you will learn to live with it. You will heal, and you will rebuild yourself around the loss you have suffered. You will be whole again, but you will never be the same. Nor should you be the same, nor would you want to.

Marv Habicht

Christopher Allen Hill
December 13, 1975 – April 24, 2013

A JOURNEY OF LOVE
IN THE MIDST OF PAIN AND SORROW

2012. Summer was here and my wife, Judy, and I had arranged to take eight days off around the Fourth of July. We were planning to make our rounds of family visits and take it easy as much as possible.

While we both grew up in Minnesota, Judy and I could be called "Hoosiers" after having spent the last two dozen years in Indiana. But we were nowhere near any of our family. Our oldest son, Chris, had settled in Champaign,

Illinois, and his brother, Tim, was in Okemos, Michigan, near East Lansing. We were building that summer's travel plans around Judy's mom's birthday celebration, and time in the Upper Midwest.

We arranged our trip in a circular route. First, we would visit Tim in Michigan and stay overnight. Then, to avoid traffic around Chicago and to enjoy the lake, we would take a ferry across Lake Michigan. From there, we'd drive as far as Madison, Wisconsin, before stopping the second night. Next day, we would head further north, and west, arriving at our destination in western central Minnesota. Our return trip to Indianapolis would bring us to Madison again. We would be in Champaign with Chris on the third of July, and back at home sometime on the Fourth.

Our journey started as planned. The ferry ride across Lake Michigan was pleasant. Soon we would check into our hotel in Madison and look for a place to have dinner. We were not far from our hotel when we received the call that would change our plans, and our lives.

Receiving a phone call meant there was news. Judy and I were baby boomers with two boys who were thirty-somethings. We were all comfortable with technology. Chris and Tim were both software developers, exposed at an early age to personal computers; but the era of smartphones did not interest them much, at least initially. We communicated only as needed. Looking back, I do remember thinking at one point, "Chris is turning into a thoughtful, nice guy who, from time to time, will call his family to check in." Again, family was important to the four of us. But, even so, it was unusual for our sons to call our cell phone while we were on the road.

Chris, in a matter of fact manner that fateful June 28, indicated he was calling from Carle Hospital in Champaign/Urbana. He had gone to the emergency room in extreme pain, had been examined by a doctor—and was told he would need colon surgery the next day (June 29).

I don't recall the details of the conversation (and I was driving, not talking). There are blurry recollections from late afternoon/early evening, June 28, going forward. For the time being, the call was ended and we told Chris we would call back. I don't remember when the "C" word (cancer) was first used.

In a state of shock, Judy and I checked into the hotel and looked for a place we could sit, get something to eat, and talk. We both knew what we needed to do. This wasn't a removal of tonsils. This was about surgery on the colon. Only later did I reflect on how this was one of the first stages of dying and grieving that were to occur. The dull, phased pain had started.

We let relatives know we needed to turn south, not north, in order to arrive in Champaign/Urbana before Chris' surgery. We called Chris to tell him of our plans, and tried to get some sleep in Madison that night. After traveling south about 250 miles the next day, we arrived at the hospital. It was an environment we had been exposed to a number of times as children or adults, but never for an extended period of time. We found our way to Chris' room and were with him for a short while before he was prepared for surgery. Prior to going in, the surgeon's nurse practitioner explained what the surgeon would be doing and what challenges could arise.

Just hearing about it was disturbing. Here was a son whom I, literally, had looked up to. I consider myself a tall person, currently about six feet three. Chris was taller than six feet ten (seven feet, in my estimation). I had forgotten the vulnerability I could feel regarding the care of this "child."

Nobody had any control over what was happening. Not Chris. Not the health care professionals. Not Judy. Not I. Lots of things went through our minds while we waited. There wasn't time to conduct our own research about removal of the colon, about the qualifications of the professionals and reputation of the hospital, about the implications of cancer in the body. I had plenty of time, during what seemed like a long, long surgery, to worry (something I don't like to do, because it is never very helpful). I did find comfort in praying over, and over, and over.

While I confess being a sinner, others tell me I'm a nice, faith-filled person. It seems, since elementary school, up until today, I have felt a value, need, and commitment to my Christian faith. I have been a Catholic over half my life. In 2010, I made my profession as a member of the Secular Franciscan Order. At the time of Chris' surgery, I had been working at Marian University in Indianapolis, a Franciscan institution which had sustained me some twenty-four years; I had started to make plans to retire after twenty-five years.

The surgeon saw us after the surgery was over. He explained that most but not all of Chris' colon had been removed. He thought he had removed the cancerous tissue, but told us in as gentle a way as possible that one can never know for sure. Pathology results were needed, along with a talk with the oncologist. The immediate task was for Chris to recover from the surgery's assault on his body.

I won't go into extensive medical details here, but it was difficult for Chris to heal. There would be days of setbacks and days of positive developments. We were in another stage of grieving. Judy and I would spend thirty-two days with Chris being in the hospital. Tim came to town for a few days so the four of us could be together. We developed routines where we would be in the room with Chris during the entire day, except when one of us would get a bite to eat. At the end of the day, with some regret, we would leave for either Chris' apartment, a local motel, or the hospital's hospitality rooms used for long-term stays, when that was possible. For the longest time in our careers, we took leave from our work and attended to only business that could be accomplished from a distance by computer.

Since the surgery had left Chris too weak to climb stairs to his third-floor apartment, we spent another seventeen days, all of us together, at an extended-stay hotel after he was discharged from the hospital. He came home to his apartment in mid-August and was strong enough for chemotherapy the third week of August. Judy, our rock through all of this time, stayed at the apartment, sleeping in Chris' bedroom, while an extra-long bed was brought into the living room for Chris. After alternating weeks between Champaign and Indianapolis, I returned to Indianapolis to attend to our home and to get some work done again. On September 13, Judy was able to return to Indianapolis, too; and on September 14, Chris was well enough to return to Wolfram Research, to the first and only full-time job he had had.

We travelled regularly to Champaign to be with Chris for medical appointments. We were there to help, to get groceries, and to be a second (and third) pair of ears to hear what the doctors were saying. It was a return to normalcy, even if it was a new normal.

In the early part of November, Judy and I flew to Minnesota for a few days to finally celebrate her mother's birthday, about four months late. Also during this time, although we had had no signs of health concerns, Judy and I followed standard medical advice for the family of someone with cancer. I had a colonoscopy in early October and Judy had hers in early December.

On December 13, Judy, Chris, and I went out to lunch to celebrate his thirty-seventh birthday. We didn't know it would get worse from there, and that the previous three months would be the best part of our thirty-six-year-old's remaining life, post-surgery.

We received a call from Chris a week later, early in the morning of December 20. He had been throwing up. Judy and I headed back to Champaign that morning. After a CT scan, the oncologist admitted Chris once again, on December 21, to Carle Hospital. He was there nine days. Tim joined us. The prescribed chemotherapy was not working. Something else was needed. (A second opinion?) If further surgery was possible, it needed to be done elsewhere. Palliative care was mentioned, but we weren't ready to discuss this.

Having grown up in Minnesota we thought about the Mayo Clinic, which had a good reputation. Chris was discharged from Carle Hospital on December 29, and we left his apartment the next day for the arduous travel to Rochester, Minnesota, in the dead of winter. Arriving on December 30, we checked into the hotel and prepared for his December 31 clinic appointment. At the conclusion of the appointment, the doctor determined Chris should be admitted to the Methodist Hospital. The Mayo doctors helped stabilize Chris' condition but did not see surgery as possible, given his circumstances. So, after a dozen days in Rochester, between the hospital and hotel room and clinic—mostly waiting for an infection to clear up—we were sent back to Champaign for a new regimen of treatment. On the way back, we stayed at the same hotel in Madison where Judy and I had stayed in June, bringing back memories of that first call from Chris.

Once we returned to Champaign, I needed to check on things in Indianapolis. But I found it hard to leave, so I wrote the following message for Judy to give to Chris:

Thursday, Jan. 24, 2013

Chris,

I love you.

The God I worship is Love. If my God took any other form but Love, I doubt that I could worship God.

Know that, no matter how imperfect, my love for you is deep. I want love to show so much of the time we share together on this earth.

I wish that I could, almost like a movie scene, put my hand on yours to draw out sorrow, pain, and illness that you suffer.

I hope that you draw upon strength that you did not know you had, that you will be responsible and show love towards the world and others in it, including yourself, your family, your health providers, and strangers.

When I was a young father, nearly 10 years younger than you, I wondered how far my love, already shown for your mom, could stretch. It is truly amazing how love, which is God, can stretch.

You are a good person.

Stretch, exercise, then be at rest and peace. Even now, there is some joy to find.

Love,
Your dad.

I returned to Indianapolis.

In Champaign, preparations were made for alternate chemotherapy treatment. The outpatient treatment started on January 30, 2013—but Chris, once again, went to the emergency room on February 20. I made another note that we were going into a new phase of the cancer; more dull pain of dying was present, even if we were not ready to name it.

Then again, two weeks later, Chris was in the hospital for about ten days and his chemotherapy treatment, scheduled for March 14, was cancelled. During Chris' hospitalization— on March 14—I received word from my brother that our ninety-four-year-old mother had died that day. I had not been to visit her as her health had started to deteriorate, because she was in South Carolina and I could not leave Champaign. So I had not been able to see her, or say goodbye. March 14 was a bad, bad day for our family. My three brothers and I decided to postpone her funeral until the summer, when many more family and friends would be able to celebrate her life.

Besides processing my mother's death, I was noticing that Chris was getting weaker and weaker. We all began contemplating options we were being forced to consider.

On March 21, Chris, Judy and I kept a previously scheduled checkup with the doctor. Only, the nature of this meeting was different from all others. After a discussion with the doctor and the rest of us, Chris decided it was time to go into a hospice program. This was one of the saddest days of our lives.

Chris knew how much of a pro-life person I was, and how I was one to never give up, regardless of the odds. I don't believe he wanted to die. He had acknowledged that this was not supposed to be happening to someone his age. When Judy went for a walk, Chris asked me if he had made the right decision about hospice. I think I must've grown through this experience, in accepting the choices others need to make for themselves, because I told him that, yes, I was a fighter, but that this was not my decision, it was his to make. The doctor had indicated that Chris probably had only four to eight weeks left; further treatment might add a few weeks—but it might also further degrade his quality of life. More than anything, I wanted Chris to know that I supported him in whatever his decision was, and I wanted him to hear that I loved him so much.

Chris stayed with his decision. Through hospice care, he was able to stay in his home, and all of us were supported by staff who tried to make Chris as comfortable as possible. Tim joined us and worked remotely, like his parents, with his computer. We all reached the conclusion that "it is what it is." Eventually, suffering will cease.

Early in the year, while he could still get out, and several weeks before going into the hospice program, Chris had purchased two tickets for the annual Ebertfest in Champaign. Ebertfest was a mid-April film festival, celebrating works selected by film critic Roger Ebert. Chris had hoped to attend with Tim. Ironically, Roger Ebert died of cancer shortly before Ebertfest. While the festival would take place without Roger, Chris would not be strong enough to go.

Chris' condition worsened, and one moment of deep pain for all of us was when he agonized aloud that he was no longer capable of walking, even in his apartment, and was limited to his hospital bed in his living room. This was the point when we, given the advice of hospice personnel, would face "do not resuscitate" orders and funeral preparations. Chris was not up to giving us direction; he thought we should approach the situation like that of an auto accident.

On the evening of April 23, Judy, Tim, and I all held onto each other, and to Chris. While he communicated with us up until this time, the room was quiet; I sensed that we were all, through tears, saying goodbye.

As had been our pattern, Tim and I left Chris and Judy and returned to the hotel, not too long before midnight. Shortly after getting to bed, we received a call from Judy. Chris had died. He died April 24, 2013, in the early, early morning. Tim and I headed back to the apartment where the four of us could be together. Judy and I, along with Tim, said goodbye to our son/brother who, only a short time before, had been fighting his fight in his own way. Per hospice instructions, they were called. It seemed we had a lot of time before anyone showed up. After the hospice person followed his standard procedures, the funeral home was contacted. Again, it seemed like a long time before they arrived. After Chris was taken away, we tried to get some sleep, as we knew we'd be needed at the funeral home later in the day.

Sometime before that night, we had been able to call a priest to meet with us and, especially, Chris. We had excused ourselves while Chris had his confession. Regardless of the nature of this process, we felt more at ease that this had taken place. However, while attempting to do the right things and be strong, I couldn't help but think science had failed us: the medical professionals could not keep Chris alive. Faith had failed us: my prayers, and the prayers of many others, could not keep Chris alive. I was angry with God. This anger has mostly receded, but every so often comes back to me.

Two days after Chris died, we received word that Judy's mother had died while hospitalized in Minnesota.

Complex funeral arrangements that we had just begun organizing for Chris were put on hold while we went to

Minnesota for Judy's mother's funeral. We eventually completed arrangements for Chris' memorial gathering at Sunset Funeral Home in Champaign on May 4, and his Mass of Christian Burial at Lakewood Cemetery in Minneapolis on May 18. We were later able to attend a hospice memorial service in Champaign on June 6, which enabled us to remember Chris among others; and we gathered at his niche wall in Minneapolis again on June 30, prior to a July 1 memorial service that was being held for my mother at another church in Minneapolis and cemetery in suburban Minneapolis.

Judy and I retired in May and June of 2013, as planned. I've heard retirement can be a singularly stressful event. But instead, it was piled on top of everything else. I had just lost my mother, Judy had just lost hers—and we both had just lost our thirty-seven-year-old son. Tim had lost his only sibling.

The hospice and funeral home people were helpful going forward. The hospice people sent us books about understanding grief, and some friends helped us make connections to hospice- and cancer-related support groups in Indianapolis. But I was not ready for them.

In the two years since, we have been engaged in handling Chris' estate, his possessions, as well as taking time to look at our own lives to see how we might simplify and disconnect from things which are not as important as relationships. Throughout the year we get regular reminders about Chris, relative to his last ten months. July 4, his birthday in December, Christmas, New Year's, and the day he died, April 24, all bring on the memories.

But Chris was more than this. And his life was more than his last months battling the sudden onset of disease. Chris was a person—a son and brother and friend—who in his thirties did not see a need to visit any doctors. He was a software engineer and lover of science. This was a very important part of his identity, and it was hard when this aspect of his identity disappeared. A friend of his, Dave Arcoleo, told us a story about Chris' first day working at Wolfram Research: Chris was being walked around the department for introductions, and while conversing, he happened to glance at someone's monitor and casually mentioned, "Shouldn't that code be like this...?" He then gave a short explanation of his idea. The guy, in amazement, recognized that Chris was correct, and that he couldn't have seen the code for more than a few seconds—all from several feet away. He confessed he had spent the entire morning trying to resolve the problem. Chris' head of the department and co-founder of the company, standing there, marveled at Chris' productivity.

Chris was a lover of film, and recollected trivia with ease, including the names of virtually every actor and director of the movies he had seen. He was an avid bicyclist who had reached the point where he didn't need to own an automobile to get around his community. Sometimes he found a ride or rented a car just to come home to Indianapolis. He was a person who thought our national political leadership, regardless of party, fell short of what it should be. He was a private person with a few strong friends.

Chris was a gatherer and rarely made the time to throw anything away. (This is a trait his dad and brother also seem to have, but not his mom.) As we have gone through his "stuff," we have connected with so many memories. Some are sad, but many bring smiles. For example, we knew how much he loved working with computers and being able to work in a field that provided meaning, but we had forgotten how long ago his interest had first presented itself.

It seems to me that tears flow more freely in my life than they used to, even relative to my predisposition to sensitivity. I have always had concern about the suffering of others. While I don't seek out pain, I consider that, when the tears come, I am going through a cleansing experience ... and this helps me see a purpose in it.... It takes me beyond the pain.

While trying to handle grief on my own, I talked with a friend from church who had similarly lost a son from cancer a number of years ago. He indicated he had connected with a group called Tuesdays with the Dads. On a cold and wintry day in January of 2014, I drove to my first 7:00 a.m. meeting. There I met Rick Larrison, whom I have discovered to be a steadfast supporter of this group. He has attended almost all Tuesday meetings, because he wants to make sure that someone is always there for anyone who might show up.

I was impressed with the stories other Dads have told about their children they have lost, and how they are handling their grief. Right away I heard about the book *Tuesday Mornings with the Dads,* and without delay following my first meeting, went to the St. Luke's United Methodist Church bookstore to purchase a copy. While it was heavy reading, I managed to get through the whole book in two days, through a lot of tears.

Since then, I have made most of our weekly meetings. I even found myself going south of Washington Street, downtown, to meet the Thursday Dads! While there are many kind people to help us, sometimes they don't understand what dads who've lost a child go through. I have found myself quietly upset when people have talked about Chris being in a better place. I am fine with him being in a better place, but would just as soon have waited several decades for this to happen, after Judy and I had died. These men, regardless of the differences in their experiences, understand. Also,

69

men and women seem to grieve differently, and I have found a bonding among men who are not afraid to share emotions and support each other.

I have come to understand that the nature of grief will change over time. I am now open to picking up those books I had previously put aside, and look forward to more meetings with others who are grieving. I now want to be there for other men, to support them.

I know that in some ways I will be grieving the rest of my life. It is now part of my life story. I am grateful for having those last ten months with Chris, even if this journey of love happened in the midst of pain and sorrow. The love continues, and life must go on.

Jack Hill

Noah Charles Kriese

October 30, 1996 – May 22, 2009

There are three mountains in the Swiss Alps that stand close together: the Eiger, the Mönch, and the Jungfrau. They are strikingly beautiful, with steep sides that round near the top, and painted with snow that swirls across the rugged terrain. On the slopes of each mountain are massive glaciers that recede in summer and grow again each winter. The debris and runoff of the glaciers meet in a single stream of frigid waters, Trümmelbach. At one point Trümmelbach drops inside a cliff wall, where it's carved a cave over many millennia. The Trümmelbachfälle—"Trümmel brook falls"— is a series of waterfalls and corkscrew chutes almost a half mile long. It carries 20,000 tons of boulders, fallen trees and other detritus through the cave each year and blasts up to 20,000 liters of water per second before it exits the mountainside and finds its way to Lake Brienz, near Interlaken. It is a wonder of natural power to behold, as the water rushes over ten waterfalls inside the cavern. It can also be terrifying.

In the valley below the mountains, is the municipality of Lauterbrunnen. In truth, it is a series of small towns; farms with steep, hilly pastures; and tall green forests. The houses are stucco and rustic wood, with tile roofs. Each house has a name carved into a calligraphic wooden sign posted on the exterior. In late spring, the pastures are covered with a quilt of red clover, Queen Anne's lace, and pink, yellow, purple, and blue wildflowers. The fragrance is intoxicating, and the flowers are officially recognized as treasures and are protected by the country and its people.

In the early morning hours a gentle symphony of bells hanging round the necks of animals in pasture breaks the chilly air. Here, in this valley with sheer cliffs on either side, the sound echoes, otherworldly and sublime.

Noah Charles Kriese

Noah came to us the day before Halloween, 1996. He was healthy and beautiful, with black hair that stuck straight out, and a peaceful nature. He was happy most of the time and was one of those kids who looks cute in every picture. He was a funny little toddler. He crawled with one leg to the side, close to his tummy, like those plastic soldiers. He loved to crawl to the CD cabinet and pull discs out, listening to the cases hit the carpet. He laughed and laughed.

When he was one, newly walking, Susan made Noah a fantastic lion costume, complete with ears, mane, and tail, and brought him to my workplace. He was a natural "ham." He couldn't speak, and could barely walk, but he waddled back and forth, roaring at all who would look. Everyone in the office loved him.

Susan was a great mother and devoted to Noah. Without fail she would read him a story, hum him a song, and rock him to sleep every night. After he had grown "too big" for rocking, she'd still read with him every night. Sometimes I'd get to read, and I wish I had done it more. Just before they go to sleep, when their minds think of what they did that day, or dream of the stories in the books, children speak the language of their nature, of the shining thoughts that are alive within them.

When Noah reached three and a half years, Susan signed him up for pee-wee soccer at the YMCA. The season is about four games long and the most excitement and focused attention come when all the kids on both teams spy the same butterfly floating onto their field.

After that, soccer was consistent in his life. We signed Noah up for spring and fall youth leagues at a nearby church. When he was old enough, we signed him up for the recreational league at Center Grove Soccer Club. Noah played other sports—baseball for a couple of seasons, four years of basketball. He had some tremendous coaches and learned a great deal from them. However, in soccer, he tried to be the best guy on the field every time, getting the most goals, or being a goalie and blocking every shot.

Susan spent hours with him practicing kicking, dribbling, stealing the ball and blocking shots. Eventually, he found his own motivation in wanting to improve himself and, as he started fifth grade, made the cut for a travel league team.

During his first year of travel soccer he played on two teams: St. Francis Rangers and the Center Grove travel B team. The Center Grove club was up a notch from St. Francis. Noah was intimidated because his teammates had more advanced ball-handling skills. He kept trying, and with each game we could see his skill and confidence improving. His coach told Noah he could be playing a lead role in defense as a fullback sweeper. It was incredible to see the ways Noah improved. He and the wing fullbacks became synchronized in their movements and communication, working as a team.

In school, Noah excelled in his studies and was well-liked by his classmates. He was creative and loved the arts, too. When he was ten he started playing electric guitar. By the second lesson he played "Smoke on the Water"—a natural. When he started sixth grade he traded his guitar for a cello. He was dedicated in his practice habits and had an exceptional ear. He could identify the notes of music he heard. We played video games together, and one evening when he was wrapping up his cello practice, I was tickled to hear him playing the theme music for *James Bond 007: GoldenEye*—the video game.

In the spring of his sixth grade year, Noah got a great opportunity. Susan's uncle Bob, a doctor of psychology, was going to lecture at Heidelberg University. He organized the trip so that family members could go along. It was going to be over two weeks in the latter part of May (2009). The trip started in Italy, with Rome and Venice; then Switzerland; and ended in Heidelberg, Germany. Susan's extended family is all very close. She made plans to go with the group and take

Noah. We checked with Noah's teachers and the school ahead of time. Given the experience and educational opportunities this would present, all were on board, with one caveat: before leaving, Noah would need to complete all the schoolwork for those two missed weeks—including the exams. Noah did it all without any problem.

Before the trip, I spent extra time with Noah. We were practicing his soccer one evening at a local football field. He wanted me to kick some really long, high kicks so that he could practice defending, heading, etc. After several kicks, he offered to teach me how to kick so that I could kick better: faster, farther. He spent more than a half hour teaching, analyzing, gently suggesting one action or way of holding my foot. I was proud of him for his patience, his tact, and his wisdom.

Just prior to the trip, Noah wanted to create a painting for Susan and asked me to coach him, since I'm a painter. Side by side, we painted a still life. He followed each step as I did it, asking advice about any technique he was unsure of. He focused on each detail with the greatest of patience and created a beautiful painting. He proudly gave it to Susan on Mother's Day. A few days later, they were on their way to Europe.

On Friday morning, May 22, I had a note on my calendar to call Noah, because he had been in Europe for a little over a week. I wanted to hear of the things he'd seen and what he thought of it all. The phone rang. It was Scott, Susan's fiancé. He said, "Kurt, I don't know how to tell you this, but Noah's missing." My ears were instantly hot and my senses became distorted—and all I could say from the center of my disbelief was, "Scott. Tell me you're lying." He told me they were in Switzerland and the police thought Noah might have fallen into the Trümmelbach waterfalls. However, they weren't completely sure—it might be possible that someone in a bus of tourists from Russia had grabbed him. He said that Susan or her cousin David would call me in an hour.

Hanging up the phone, all I could say was, "Oh my god. Oh my god." At that time, my son Jacob was living with me. He heard me and came to see what had happened. I told him what Scott had said. Jacob immediately set about trying to focus my racing mind. He asked whether my passport was current. I called Senator Lugar's office, explained that my son was missing in another country, and asked what I could do to renew my passport—my voice shaking the whole time.

In the meantime Jacob had called his sister, Rachel; his mother and stepfather (Suzanne and Ted); my mother; my sister Cindy and her daughters, Jennifer and Jill. We prayed for Noah that all would turn out to be okay. But by this time it was more than three hours after Noah had gone missing.

On the second call, Susan's cousin David indicated that the police were leaning toward the possibility that Noah had fallen into the falls, but were handling it as a missing-person case for now.

Noah was a very responsible twelve-year-old who didn't take crazy risks. He wore a helmet when riding his bicycle and reminded everyone to "buckle up" in the car. None of this made any sense.

The other possibility—of Noah being abducted—was chilling and disturbing in so many ways. I wanted neither of these options.

Senator Lugar's office called. They had set in motion the process for renewing my passport and said the embassy in Bern was aware of the situation. My niece Jennifer made copies of my documents and credit cards, created a schedule for me to follow with specific instructions, and coordinated my passport and flight requirements with my brother Chris, who lives in San Francisco. Chris immediately took time off from his job and arranged to meet me in Zürich.

En route to Switzerland, I tried to focus on doing what I needed to do next, but waves of sadness and concern for Noah's safety were relentless.

Arriving at the hotel just after noon, the first thing I noticed was a "missing person" poster for Noah, taped to the front door. The police had used photos from Susan's camera. One photo of his face was large and so current that it took my breath away. These posters were on every business window and community board in town. Susan met us in the lobby and told me what little they knew at that point. We would be briefed by the police later.

In the meantime, David took us to Trümmelbach Falls, where Noah had last been seen and where he and Noah had last spoken. They had been near the top viewing platform, when he told Noah the attraction was closing and that they needed to leave. Noah had indicated he would follow.

There are tunnels and stairs that follow the course of the waters through the cave. At any given time, there may be two or three rows of people peering over each other at the falls, and there is much traffic of people ascending and descending the stairs. It can be difficult to keep track of another person. When David noticed that Noah was not behind him, he figured Noah had walked past. However when David got to the exhibit entrance and met Susan and other family members at a predesignated spot, Noah wasn't there. They thought, at first, that he must have gone to the parking lot. He wasn't there, either. They stood at the entrance—a single turnstile—until everyone had left. They were allowed to go back into the attraction and look once more. There was no sign of him. The police were called.

The police interviewed the people who worked at the attraction, as well as all the family members. The man who ran the elevator had heard people from a Russian tour bus talking about an American boy and his shoe. However, he wasn't sure what they were specifically saying and, at the time, there hadn't been cause for him to intentionally eavesdrop. The police put out the Swiss equivalent of an all-points bulletin, but an APB was about all they could do.

Noah had disappeared and there were no witnesses. A woman from New Zealand thought she saw someone go by in the water, but her husband had been looking elsewhere and couldn't confirm it. The woman was shaken up and wasn't completely certain of what she had seen, but it was enough for the police to suspect that Noah might have slipped into the water. They called the Swiss Alpine Rescue team.

David said it was like watching an action movie, with the Alpine Rescue rappelling the cave walls, and helicopters tracing the path of the river along its twenty kilometer journey to Lake Brienz.

We went back to the hotel to meet with a detective, Terese, who had been assigned to investigate. She explained that they didn't have anything to show us or that could indicate, for certain, where Noah was. A floating barrier had been erected across the entrance to Lake Brienz. If Noah had fallen into the falls, his body might eventually arrive there. They offered to take us there.

At Lake Brienz, a series of large yellow inflatable cylinders were connected, stretching across the mouth of the river. I asked Terese whether I could walk the banks of the river between the lake and the falls, to look for some sign of Noah. She tried to discourage me. But, since there was no way to help with the other possibility—abduction—I told my brother, Susan, and Scott that that's what I was going to do, starting the minute we got back to the hotel. They came along, too.

We worked systematically, starting up by the falls, then working toward the lake. We walked on the northwest side of the river, since it offered clear access and we could see both banks from there. The stream was twenty feet wide, a few feet deep, and very rapid. Seeing nothing to let us know Noah's fate, I prayed as we walked along: "Please, just give us some clue to let us know where you are. If you're in the falls, let us know. Or let the police find that bus." Just moments later, as we approached the falls, Chris yelled, "Look! A shoe in the falls!" We saw something black hit the river water and raced to retrieve it. The fast water carried it past Chris and me, but Scott grabbed it on his second attempt. We were soaked and wet, but the object had been captured. Any satisfaction at the capture was completely overwhelmed by examining it and realizing it was indeed our Noah's shoe.

The police arrived quickly and took the shoe into evidence. While Susan was talking to them by the entrance to the falls, my brother and I stood for a time on the opposite side of the river, waiting, in case anything else came from the falls.

The leader of the Alpine Rescue team, Fritz, arrived. He used a backhoe to move boulders and dirt to form a better barrier around the net he had stretched across the stream. His wife, Sonja, came out with a long pole configured to grab objects. She stood in the cold wet spray of the stream for more than three hours, peering at the water. She stood there, waiting, in solidarity and compassion for people from another country. She wouldn't leave until darkness forced us all to leave.

The next day Chris and I walked the two miles of stream bank between town and the falls. We climbed over and under fences. We looked for any evidence of Noah. Our shoes and clothing were soaked by a constant drizzle and inadvertent slips into the water.

Back in Indianapolis, my daughter, Rachel, had created a Facebook group called "Urgent Prayers Needed: Noah Kriese." The prayers and messages posted by family, friends, and people in the community helped our sagging spirits.

On Tuesday evening we held a prayer service near the entrance to the falls. It was a simple service, with a few words from an Anglican minister vacationing in the nearby village of Wengen.

Trying to understand what we faced, we asked the owner of the Trümmelbach attraction when the stream might slow down enough to recover Noah. He said probably the following October, when the glaciers started to freeze again.

On Wednesday, Chris had to leave, returning to his job. My son Jacob arrived to take his place. For the next three days, and well into each night, Jacob and I walked the stream, looking for signs of Noah. Our feet and our hearts were soaked and weary.

Mark, the hotel owner, made us food hours after the kitchen had closed. He and his wife, Ursula, are especially generous and kind people. He had driven the five-hour round trip to the airport and picked us up. They gave us the use of a large special-event room to meet in all week, filled a huge basket with fruit, bread, jellies and treats, and placed a candle with a picture of Noah in the lobby of the hotel.

Friday brought further evidence of what had happened to Noah. We were called to the local police station and shown a pair of black shorts. They were shredded with long vertical rips, as if someone had taken a machete to them. They were Noah's. The sight of them brought further realization of the physical assault on his body by the water in the falls. Being completely focused on searching for my son, it hadn't registered in my consciousness what tremendous forces would have been exerted on his body. I thought of him struggling against the power of such forces, if he had survived a fall into the water, and I wept. My son Jacob held his arm around my shoulder. He was shaken, too.

I still weep at the thought, six years later. Noah was a fighter. The thought of him struggling against such force sends waves of sadness through me. "Brutal" is too soft a word to describe the natural forces at work. Noah was a good and loving son, a good friend to many, and generous in spirit. He did not deserve that.

Each morning at 5:00 a.m., when the water was shallower due to the cooling night air, Fritz, the Alpine Rescue leader, did a walk-through of the falls. He searched for any sign of Noah before the crowds of people came through. It was Fritz who had found Noah's shorts.

The water level in the cave changes from one day to the next. Though we could walk through the cave and clearly see the water as it raced through the shallower parts, the dark recesses held their secrets and our Noah. After several cool nights in succession, the water level dropped a bit. The police divers and the Alpine Rescue team allowed a few of their members to descend the slick wet surfaces of the cave walls to points just above the water's surface. They used long flexible poles to poke the darker, deeper spots. It was a slow, painstaking process. They looked for three hours, but there was no sign of Noah. Our best hope of finding Noah prior to the warm summer thaw, was gone.

Sometimes we don't have clear answers about what happens in life, or why an end to life occurs.

What happened to Noah, as nearly as we can discern, is this: after David talked to him, Noah started to descend a long set of stairs from the top platform. As he was walking, he apparently tripped—and lost one of his shoes, which landed on the rock surface outside of a guard rail. Looking at the rock from directly above, in the indirect light of the cave, it doesn't look steep. Noah probably thought he could reach the shoe. However, viewing the surface from the side, one can see that the rock is extremely steep. Noah probably tried to reach his shoe through the railing, and slipped. The silt and mist of the waterfalls create a slick surface on the rock. The spot where he apparently fell drops fifty feet, with large boulders protruding from the cave floor in a powerful swirl of water. I wondered how the other visitors in the cave could not see or notify someone of what they had seen. But even if someone had witnessed Noah slip, and reported it, the reality is that probably nothing could have changed the outcome once he fell.

After returning to Indianapolis, we started to plan Noah's celebration of life gathering for June 19–20, 2009. The people of the Center Grove community and Emmanuel Church of Greenwood, the church that Noah attended, opened their arms and gave us much time and support in planning everything.

The Tuesday prior to the memorial, Susan received a call from Terese, the Swiss detective. On his morning rounds, Fritz had found Noah's body. It would take a week for the authorities in Bern to conduct an autopsy, then have his body prepared for shipment and transported to Zurich for a flight.

The outpouring of love for Noah at the celebration-of-life was beautiful. His soccer teammates were ushers, manning the doors despite their own sadness and grief. The Center Grove High School orchestra played music that soothed as much as anything could. The love and statements of family and friends carried us all through this time of grief.

The following Tuesday, I rode in a hearse to Chicago to pick up my son at the airport. It was deeply unsettling to see a sign with the words "human remains" attached to the crate that held my son. The funeral home employee who was driving the hearse removed the outer crate to reveal the beautiful birchwood coffin that held Noah's body. Laying my arm over the part of the coffin where Noah's feet were positioned, I knew he was "there" … in the coffin, and with me in spirit … for that ride home.

Three days later, we had a small funeral service and laid him to rest. It felt that Noah was at rest, finally, in the soil of his home. The unreality of losing my son, however, would take a long time to settle in. Every morning, for at least six months, I would wake and subconsciously listen for my son stirring in the next room. And hear nothing. Then, I would remember that Noah was gone, and that this terrible dream was my reality, and I would weep. I made a conscious decision to allow myself to mourn Noah for however long it took.

In August of that year I received a phone call from Brian Elo. He had lost his fourteen-year-old son, Ben, only a year earlier. Like Noah, Ben was quite a good soccer player. Brian said that it might be helpful to have a cup of coffee and chat. When we got together he told me about Ben's passions and interests. He shared some of the circumstances of his son's passing. My face was wet with tears as I heard his story and then tried to share some of mine. Brian told me about the Mornings with the Dads group, which had started to meet at a location near me. I was reluctant to consider this at first, not sure that anything would help in healing me. However, I agreed to attend a breakfast meeting. The men welcomed me, and then, one by one, shared verbal portraits of their children and the stories of their passing. As they spoke, wetness appeared on most men's eyes, but there was no discomfort about this in anyone present. There was no shame, only the love for a child, that we each felt and knew.

I'll be mourning Noah for as long as I breathe. But the healing that makes living manageable comes from the graces given and received from friends and family, especially my wife, Michele; son, Jacob; and daughter, Rachel.

Kurt Kriese

Jennifer Lynn Buxton Longworth
January 22, 1976 – November 10, 2012

Jennifer Lynn Buxton Longworth is the oldest of our three children. At the date of her death, she was thirty-six years old. Her brothers, Jed and Joe, were thirty-three and twenty-five years old, respectively. The night she was killed, the spirit of our family was forever altered. I miss her more than I could ever have imagined.

Jenny enjoyed a typical childhood: dance classes, Brownies, Cabbage Patch dolls, Debbie Gibson and little brothers. She studied dance for ten years and joined band in middle school. In high school, she earned a first chair for flutes in one of the orchestras and was in the state champion marching band. It was a parental thrill watching her march in competition with over a hundred other band members. Marching band was also the mainstay of her high school social life. I will always carry my picture of her wearing her band letter jacket. It is the one she wanted me to have.

Losing a child causes one to think about what you didn't do or say at the right moment. We wish we could go back and replay those times, but cannot. I suppose I have asked myself these questions a thousand times. Did she know how much we loved her and appreciated her for the person she was? Did she understand that she belonged to her mother and me first, last and always—and how in love with her we were? No matter how I try to get a YES from myself, I am starting to realize I will always carry that smallest piece of doubt.

Jenny graduated from Ball State University with her elementary teaching degree, earned her teaching license, and was fortunate enough to gain employment with the Greenwood Community School Corporation. She was a member of the second grade teaching team at Southwest Elementary for eleven years. She made good friends there and they have become friends of ours. In 2009, she completed her Master of Education at Indiana Wesleyan University—with a 4.0, by the way. It was a wonderful day when we went to the main campus to attend her graduation. We have some great pictures of her and Dion sharing the victory. She would be the first to say his support allowed her to concentrate on the task at hand. I don't recall them ever not being supportive of each other's career.

Jenny met Dion Longworth while both were working their way through college, working summer jobs at the mall. They dated about three years and she was thrilled when they got engaged. They announced their engagement at Christmastime, 1999. I am confident it was her best Christmas ever. They were married on July 7, 2001, at St. Barnabas Catholic Church, with Father J. Joseph McNally (Father Mac) officiating. Father Mac retired in 2002 and passed away on October 10, 2012—exactly one month before Jenny and Dion were killed. And Jesus said, "In my Father's house there are many mansions: if it were not so, I would have told you. I go to prepare a place for you" (John 14:2). When Father Mac died, Jenny made certain I saw his obituary. He closed his Mass with the Irish Blessing, and that held a lot of meaning for Jenny. The end of the Irish Blessing, as Fr. Mac said it, was, " … and until we meet again, may God hold you in the hollow of his hand." That is inscribed on Jenny and Dion's headstone.

Jenny and Dion purchased their home in Richmond Hill in the summer of 2004. Once they had their home, they entered into the family holiday rotation. We went to their home each second or third Thanksgiving. Christmas Eve after Mass, she would have a light meal and we would open one gift … normally another tree ornament.

I believe what makes the holidays so difficult after a death, is that we establish traditions with a "forever" expectation, which is the only way it can be—and traditions revolve around family, whether in general or regarding a specific family member. When a specific person is no longer physically here, that holiday and the associated traditions may become a burden or even untenable, especially in the years immediately following the loss. We never thought we would have so few Christmas Eves, birthdays, wedding anniversaries, or holidays with Jenny and Dion. Not only is the loss of the special day devastating, the *loss of expectation* of the special day is devastating. Who doesn't look forward to the day itself several days or weeks before?

Jenny loved to cook and bake, and she was continually bringing new creations to us. We had a small business in Greenwood, not much more than a mile from Jenny's school. She would occasionally stop in on her way home to bring us up to date, or to let us sample a new recipe. She and I had some of our best philosophical discussions during those visits. It has come to us that the little things—the impromptu visit, the quick phone call or text message, the missed-call followed by her voice message—have as much importance as any big event. For months after she was killed, we would expect a phone call that normally would have been made but wasn't. She might see something on TV and call her mom and start with, "Did you see...?" Of course, the girl-talk between mother and daughter is forever lost. Now the comment is, "Jenny would have loved this—" or, "Jenny would have hated that...."

My wife, Nancy, and I have attended funerals for her grandparents, her father, my grandparents, my parents and a younger brother, aunts, uncles and friends. I had no idea what a loss through death was until November 10, 2012. I have been trying to find words to define the feeling. Loss, despair, frustration, denial. The list can go on endlessly. I keep coming back to EMPTY. I have truly loved those who have died; but the inside-out feeling, the emptiness that crept across me the night Jenny was killed, has remained.

I have taken to reading the "Remembrance" section in the newspaper obituaries. It helps me understand and accept that there will forever be a hole in my heart and life that only Jenny could fill. When I read that a dad had lost his seventeen-year-old son, and that it had happened forty-five years ago—and I could still read the total grief in his expression of love—I started to realize there is no healing, just acceptance. Acceptance that Jenny is gone, and acceptance of knowing how horrible the emptiness is and that it is here to stay.

I don't think one person can tell another person how he (or she) should deal with the loss of a child. That person can tell only how *he* is dealing with the loss of his child. About three months after Jenny was killed, I began meeting with a group of fathers—the "Dads" in this book—who have lost a child or even two. Some have been coping with the loss for a year or less, and some are going on twenty years. I am learning that the Dads have both similar and different experiences in dealing with child-loss grief. But I believe they agree that it is a grief different from any other type of grief they have met.

Saturday, November 10, 2012, was a pleasant day in Indianapolis, Indiana. The weather was warm for early November, and the evening was perfect for one more stroll walking the dog or playing outside with the kids until late. Then, a few minutes after 11:00 p.m., the heinous act that quickly became known as the Richmond Hill Explosion took place—thirteen feet north of our daughter and son-in-law's home—and our family's world was ripped apart.

Nancy and I had been following the 11:00 news when the story broke about a massive explosion on the south side of Indianapolis. An update located it near Jenny and Dion's subdivision, so we tried their cell phones—then the land line—then the cell phones again. When news reports pinpointed the explosion in the 8400 block of Fieldfare Way, in the Richmond Hill subdivision, we got a very sick feeling. As I recall, at this time I called 911 and gave them specific information about the number of people living at 8355

Fieldfare Way. In a short while, between 12:30 and 1:00 a.m., November 11, Dion's father, John, called Nancy and me and said we needed to go to Mary Bryan Elementary School for more information.

Mary Bryan Elementary School was northeast of Richmond Hill and had become the command center for the police and fire departments, homeland security, and the Red Cross. Nonresident family members could go there and hopefully get information about, and even reunite with, loved ones. As we made the ten-minute drive from our home, we rationalized to ourselves that the kids were alright, just not able to receive calls, because of the home's damage. When we walked up to the information desk in the gym, they asked about our relationship to Richmond Hill. We told them our daughter's address, and the fire department information officer's face became pale. They whisked us into the teachers' lounge. It was just us and Dion's father at that point. We spent the next five to six hours waiting for information that never came. People would come in and ask us if we needed anything like coffee, water, a sandwich. At one point they asked again if they could do anything for us, and we asked them to contact the priests at St. Barnabas. Reality was creeping into our thoughts.

We would ask about our kids, and the answers were generally vague and evasive. They had to make one hundred percent certain before telling us the bodies they had found were our children. That happened about daybreak, when a troop of chaplains, fire, and coroner's office personnel came in and sat down with us. I don't remember their words, but I remember what they meant. They were asking permission to obtain dental records ... because the damage done had made our children unrecognizable.

90

I remember crying, then trying to regain composure, then crying more. We had spent the whole night wanting to believe our children would appear. Reality has arrived.

In piecing together what we now know, we believe our Jenny had been preparing for, or in, bed; and that our son-in-law, Dion, had been "closing the house down for the evening," and was either already in, or blown into, the basement when the explosion took place. They were the two people closest to what is believed to be a contrived natural-gas explosion that immediately destroyed homes—and caused so much damage that thirty-plus houses, out of eighty-plus damaged houses in the neighborhood, had to have major structural repair and/or total replacement before the homes could again be safely occupied. The "what ifs" are endless. If they had gone to a movie, been visiting family or friends, been out walking Pepper, their beautiful Golden Collie (assuming they would have been far enough away from the explosion). We know the "what ifs" could have gone the other way. What if friends or family members had been visiting them?

When I replay that night, two things stand out in my mind. We spent the night in a teachers' lounge—and our Jenny was a teacher. And, we spent the night hoping and praying, even though our children's time of death was later established as 11:14 p.m. I don't confuse that time with the time of the determination. The determination may have been made days later, after the autopsies. What haunts me is that they were dead probably even before we heard the first news report. I understand that the powers that be were not prepared to say anything until they did, but it sometimes seems like a long torturous night that could have been shortened.

When we left the school, the police officers escorted us away from the press. We cried all the way home and all that day and for the weeks and months that have followed. In the meantime, we had to deal with the business of death.

Our sons had not been present at the school that night. Jed was in northern Indiana visiting his in-laws, and Joe was in southern Indiana on a weekend camping trip. The press were already starting to put names on the news, so I felt I had to tell Jenny's brothers with phone calls so they wouldn't hear it on the radio or TV. I remember the disbelief in my voice and theirs. They were at our house within about three hours. Then, I would call one of my siblings and tell the news—and while I would try to recover for my next call, my wife would make one of hers. I had to make three calls, she had to make five. Nancy's mother had been living with us since mid-September of 2012. Her husband of sixty-five years had died in August and we were adjusting to his passing. She, especially. We were able to delay telling her until later in the day. It went as you might expect.

One of the tougher non-family calls came about midmorning Sunday, when the principal at Jenny's school called and said, "Mr. Buxton, I have a classroom full of teachers with me and we need to talk to you." I believe they already knew the story, but she needed to confirm it so she and the staff could plan for Monday and beyond. We will always be thankful to the staff at Southwest Elementary for the compassion they showed Jenny and us, and Jenny's students, during this entire ordeal. The principal told me later that when she walked into Jenny's classroom that Sunday to get a handle on things, everything was already in place for the new week. Jenny worked on the basis that, if she got sick or couldn't be at school the next day, for whatever reason, she didn't want the substitute teacher or the children to be lost. She had even placed a little gift on the desk of a student who was having a birthday that Monday.

Another tougher call came that Sunday morning from Jenny's closest girlfriend. I answered the phone, she introduced herself and asked how Jenny was doing. She knew about the explosion but was unaware of the result. I replied that Jenny and Dion were dead. She screamed, there was silence, and then she hung up. She later told us that she, Jenny, and Dion had gone to a movie that Saturday afternoon and had then gotten a bite to eat. She had been with them hours before they were killed.

We turned the news off during that first day. It seemed every television station in town went to Jenny's Facebook page and used her and Dion's wedding picture to lead with, when starting a report. We were in no man's land in our lives, and we kept seeing a picture of our daughter on the happiest day of her life, being used as a lead-in for how she had died. They'd show the roaring fire in the black of night—and we would see our children's bodies being decimated by the fire.

Several days after Jenny and Dion's home was demolished by the explosion, then engulfed in flames, I had a chance to be escorted onto the property to see what I might find. The explosion had been so destructive that investigators were finding things in the basement, and on the property, that had come from several houses away. We soon realized that if we found anything, it probably wouldn't be Jenny and Dion's, because their personal possessions were gone. Even Pepper, their dog, was never found. She was extremely well-behaved, and a love of their life. They had done the chip implant in case she was ever lost, but her whereabouts are unknown to this day. There were no canine remains in the fire—and trust me, the investigators used a sifter going through the debris. So I was not looking for any valuables. I was hoping to find a memory, a keepsake. I was so desperate to find something, I was picking up charred bricks that had been on the front of their home.

While I was there, there were several insurance investigators at the site, looking for whatever they could find. Not knowing who I was, one of them came up to me and asked me if I knew who the girl was in the picture he had found. It was Jenny, beaming, standing in our front yard with her prom date, her junior year in high school. I took the picture, and cried.

It was nine days from the day Jenny and Dion were killed, until the day we could bury their remains. Sometimes it seems like days, sometimes months. The two families had honored the couple's decision to spend their lives together. And now their ashes are forever together. That was the one decision made for us. Their bodies were so damaged by the explosion and fire that cremation was necessary. We never got that visual goodbye.

At night my wife and I would lie down in bed, hold hands and cry. I can't remember when that started to ease off a little, but it was well after the funeral. It hasn't stopped, just slowed.

Jenny and Dion were the two fatalities of this atrocity. If you care to read more about it, web-search "Richmond Hill Explosion" or "Jennifer and Dion Longworth, explosion victims." As of August, 2015, there have been five con-spirators arrested. One trial has ended, resulting in a life sentence without parole. (An appeal has been requested.) A second conspirator has entered a plea bargain in exchange for testimony against the others, and will be sentenced when all other conspirators have had their day in court. The next trial is slated to begin in early 2016, and the last two sometime after. The nightmare that started in November, 2012, will continue, in one form or another, forever.

My wife and I want to thank our neighbors, friends, family members, Jenny's and Dion's coworkers, St. Barnabas staff, funeral home staff, and others who continue to support and grieve with us for Jenny and Dion.

While our family goal in writing Jenny's story is to tell about her too-short life, her contributions to her students, and what our ongoing grief journey has been like, we would be remiss not to recognize that Dion's death is an integral part of our grief for Jenny. He was by her side for one third of her life. As parents of the bride, we were happy that she selected exactly the kind of man we would have wished for her. Dion loved her beyond condition and was an excellent provider with an outstanding work ethic. He supported her teaching career without reservation. He had a terrific sense of humor and could give as well as he took when the joking started. He would come to your aid no matter what the need may be. His last thoughts on this earth were about our daughter and her well-being. We know this because the last first-responder to speak to him, seconds before the fire consumed him, has told us Dion's last words were of Jenny.

Our sons, Jed and Joe, have been our rocks who have gotten us through this, thus far. They have been at our sides, comforting us with their presence. They have loved us, cried with us, hugged us, and have reminded us what fine men they are and how much Jenny means to them, too. We are so thankful for them. And for Jed's darling wife, Diana, and their son, Oliver. Jed and Diana were expecting our family's first grandchild at the time of this tragedy. Oliver was born about three months after Jenny's death. Diana is a wonderful daughter-in-law and mother, and has been a terrific source of support for all of us.

A special thank you, also, to Jenny's students, who are now somewhere between third grade and college age. The pictures, stories, cards, handshakes and hugs we received from them during that week, and since, have been a blessing. Their teachers organized all of those gifts and we have saved each one. And to those staff members who expressed such love for Jenny, we thank you so much. We can never explain what that means to our entire family. The Southwest Elementary Parent Teacher Organization has honored Jenny and Dion with the Southwest Elementary Jennifer and Dion Longworth Memorial Award. Please read more about Jenny as a teacher, and the award honoring her and Dion, at www.gws.k12.in.us. Click on the "Home" tab and then on "Southwest Elem. School." Once in the Southwest Elementary School site, click on "Southwest Information," currently on the right side of the page. It will show a link to the Jennifer and Dion Longworth Memorial Award. Otherwise, an Internet search will lead to the information.

A last thought about our Jenny and what her teaching meant to the school community. Early in her career, she made a decision to give every student a Christmas gift, made by her. She knitted scarves for the girls and hats for the boys. Each gift had the initials of the recipient so the kids would know they were special to her. We found a picture Jenny had taken a few days before the explosion, showing the Christmas gifts, completed and wrapped and ready for delivery. They were destroyed in the explosion. Volunteers from the Southwest Elementary staff, parents, and the Greenwood community remade those gifts, including the initials. I can imagine the tears that are in those gifts. I remember crying about it when the story was aired on the news—for the sadness of losing her, and for the generosity of others in replacing those gifts, but also because it reminded me how Jenny never wanted someone else to do her work.

But Jenny wouldn't have wanted the gifts to be given in sadness. It's the LOVE that was, and continues to be, important … the love she felt for the children, and also the love that was shown by the volunteers who made sure the children received the gifts as she had intended. Putting the kids first. I would almost bet it was the first time Jenny was ready that far in advance … and then, to have it destroyed. But because she had done that, and had had a picture taken, others knew to replace them.... Her caring instinct as a teacher continued to bless her students even after she was gone.

As I write this, Southwest Elementary has completed a large facility expansion, including a new media center. They have dedicated the new center in Jenny's honor and have placed a plaque with her name and picture at the entrance. These words are inscribed at the bottom of the plaque, below her picture; they also appear prominently across the front wall of the center:

We all need someone who inspires us
to do better than we know how.
                              —Anonymous

Our family is so thankful that our Jenny has been remembered in this way by the school she was so dedicated to, and the children she so loved, and that she will be known by the children of the future, as well.

Don Buxton

John "Dion" Longworth
June 22, 1978 – November 10, 2012

A cardinal was singing in a tree just outside the open window of the room where Dion was born at 3 p.m. on June 22, 1978. The windows of that room at Ball Memorial Hospital opened onto a courtyard. I left for a meeting shortly thereafter and returned that evening to find Dion's mother, Elaine, holding him. He turned his eyes in my direction and smiled when I said, "Hello" and asked him how he was doing. It seems he spent most of his life smiling.

Dion always amazed me with his attitude and his approach to life. He worked hard to succeed and was usually correct in his belief that he could do virtually anything if he really wanted to. He learned to read before he was three years old and seemed to learn at will. The summer he turned three he used a screwdriver to disassemble our stereo turntable, and neither he nor I could ever get it to work again. For

Dion's first eight years, we lived and worked on my family's dairy farm. Life on the farm developed in Dion an appreciation and love of nature. In the many hours Dion spent with my father, he learned to love gardening. This love carried into his adult desire to turn his entire yard into a garden. One spring, when I was inspecting the farm with Elaine and our three children, Dion ran ahead of us. We soon heard him loudly exclaim, "Onions!" When we arrived at his location, we learned that the four-year-old had discovered cattails by a creek. On an earlier occasion, when he was three, Dion had been watching me clean out a silage conveyer when I pulled out a garter snake that was about three feet long. I dropped it on the ground near Dion and he immediately picked it up to look at it. It attempted to bite him, but he was not concerned. I had him drop it in a bucket and sent him to the house to show it to his mother. Minutes later, I heard a scream. Dion did not understand why his mother was upset.

Dion's greatest gift was his commitment to love and appreciate everyone. He was born with the ability to communicate his love well, with respect and appreciation for everyone he met. Dion was small for his age, until he grew several inches during the summer between ninth and tenth grade. Before he grew taller, he had faced the potential dilemma of being bullied. He managed those situations by learning how to talk to the bullies—and most of them decided to be his friends, instead. When he was six years old, Dion worked with me at the county fair as a volunteer at the Democrat booth. He was to give away Walter Mondale stickers from a large roll. In Randolph County, the Democrats do not get many visitors. While I was occupied with one, Dion noticed that, about sixty feet away, the Republicans were giving away popcorn to a long line of people. He walked over to the line and began giving everyone a Mondale sticker to place on their bags of popcorn. Dion distributed several hundred of the stickers that night.

Elaine and I divorced when Dion was nine years old. Eventually, Elaine, Dion, and Dion's younger sister, Brookley, moved to Henderson, Kentucky, the home of the largest high school in Kentucky. The growth spurt that had occurred between the ninth and tenth grades had resulted in surgery on both of Dion's knees. The doctor told him he would not be able to run again, but I bought a bicycle for him to use to rehabilitate his legs during his tenth grade year—and in his junior year, Dion made the varsity cross country team and ran in the Kentucky state cross country meet. In his senior year, he was vice president of his class.

Dion had a lifelong love of electronics. In his early teens, he discovered one of the world's leading audio speaker manufacturers—Klipsch—was located in Indianapolis, and he began dreaming of working there. After graduating high school, Dion moved to Indianapolis to live with me and attend Indiana University-Purdue University Indianapolis (IUPUI) as an electrical engineering student. He joined the cross country team his freshman year and was active in several student organizations. He had planned to transfer to the Purdue campus at West Lafayette for his junior year, but those plans were derailed when he met his future wife, Jennifer Buxton. She and Dion were working their way through college at the Montgomery Ward in Greenwood Park Mall. Frequently, I would have lunch or supper with Dion at the mall. One day, he asked me to follow him through the store. We arrived in the clothing section, where he introduced me to my shy future daughter-in-law, Jennifer.

When it was time for his senior project in college, he contacted Klipsch. He arranged an agreement in which he,

101

leading a team of four electrical engineering students, would develop a product for the company. Klipsch management liked their work and hired them following graduation.

Dion and I often met for lunch on Thursdays, and planned several weekend activities each year. The last time we had lunch was on Thursday, November 1, 2012.

The following week, I called Dion several times. I had hoped to have lunch with him or meet on the weekend.

On Saturday, November 10, I attended a Butler basketball game with a friend. I had experienced flu symptoms during the day, and by 9:30 that evening, I was feeling quite ill and went to bed early. ... Just after 11 p.m., my teenage grandson, Tylor, called, asking if we had felt an earthquake or something that would have caused his house to shake. I tell him no and attempt to return to sleep. A couple of minutes later he calls again to say there has been a report on TV of an explosion in the 8400 block of Fieldfare Way. Dion's address is 8355 Fieldfare Way, so I dress quickly and head south. Adrenaline kicks in.

I arrive at the intersection of Sherman Drive and Stop 11 Road to see an angry policeman waving and yelling at me to turn west. I would later regret that I did not drive around him. Ever since the shock and adrenaline of that night wore off, I have wished that I had driven past the officer to get as close to the house as possible. But, instead, I circle around to Mary Bryan Elementary School, where people are gathering. My wife, Dotsie, calls to tell me the authorities want people to go to the school to meet loved ones. Dion's older sister, Emily, also calls, to say she and Tylor are already there.

On the way into the school, I see flames and smoke rising about a quarter of a mile away, in the vicinity of Dion's home. A crowd mills about the gymnasium. I search for Dion and Jennifer, but don't find them. I ask the officer in charge of taking names if either of them is listed. He answers, "No." At some point, someone tells us there are four hospitals where those injured in the explosion have been taken. We leave to visit hospitals but do not find Dion or Jennifer. At this point I am regretting that I didn't park the car and run across the schoolyard to Dion's house.

I return to the school, where a chaplain tells me that Dion's house is at "ground zero" of the explosion. There are reports that one person has been confirmed dead. We do not want to accept that it could be Dion or Jennifer. By this time, Emily and Tylor have been directed to a nearby church where people are gathering. I meet them there and we continue to hope that Jennifer and Dion will appear. The crowd at the church thins until there are only fire and police department personnel with us. We return to the school, where a few fire and police officials are present, along with a large number of the media. I call Dotsie, Jennifer's parents, and Dion's mother and younger sister (Brookley), and suggest they come to the school.

We wait at the school all night for a report from the fire department.

Sunday morning, at about 8:00, we are told that Dion and Jennifer were found lying next to each other on their bed, where it had fallen into the basement at the north end of the house. In shock, Dotsie and I leave, stopping by our church on the way home.

Finally, we go home, and collapse in exhaustion.

Dotsie was busy for days intercepting news media calls. She has been very responsive to my daughters, grandchildren, and others throughout the aftermath of this tragedy. I know my grief has been difficult for her and I am thankful for her presence.

The first week was a blur. We spent much time talking to a funeral director, family, police, friends, the coroner, and an insurance company. Elaine, Dion's mother, visited the fire station where she was told again that Dion and Jennifer had been found together, in their bed.

The funeral visitation was eight days after the explosion. We accepted visitors for at least eight hours. At about six hours into the gathering, we met two of Dion's neighbors, the Hollingsworths, who claimed they had been with Dion when he died—and that they had spoken with him. We thought they were crazy, since the fire department had told us Dion had died next to Jennifer in their bed. Over the next few weeks, we would learn that the Hollingsworths' story was nearer to the truth.

A more complete story of Dion's death has since emerged. We have learned that two or three minutes after the explosion, these two neighbors approached the rear of Dion's house. The second story of the house had collapsed completely. Flames were rapidly spreading, but the neighbors drew close and yelled into the rubble, asking if anyone was in the house. They heard Dion banging around, and then saw his face appear in an opening in the rubble. He was moving about and appeared to be in good condition in his basement workshop. The house had an escape portal in the basement, but it was blocked by debris which was unable to be removed. At the southwest corner of the house, the chimney had fallen away from the south wall of the house, leaving a gap between the living room floor and the wall. The gap was too small to allow Dion to escape, but they were able to talk to him through it. Dion told them Jennifer was upstairs in the bedroom and asked his rescuers to help her first. During the rescue attempt, Dion repeatedly asked about Jennifer, and whether anyone was helping her. He did not know the initial explosion had collapsed the entire north end of the house and set it ablaze.

About five minutes after the explosion, the first fire crew had arrived from a station that was about a quarter of a mile away as the crow flies. Soon after arriving, the lieutenant in charge of the crew stepped inside Dion's front door and called out to see if anyone was in the house, but he did not hear anybody respond.

Several other neighbors joined the rescue effort as the firefighters deployed in the area in front of the house. One of the neighbors was a retired police captain who went to the front of the house to get help from the firefighters. Another was an off-duty firefighter without any protective gear. Yet another was an off-duty policeman who used his radio to communicate with the fire department. At least one other neighbor also tried to help.

Perhaps ten minutes after the explosion, two firefighters began removing debris from over Dion. The IFD battalion chief soon arrived and was standing in Dion's backyard frantically calling on the radio for more help. A fireman tried to work his way to Dion's location with a hose, but gas leaks were feeding the flames between the two houses—so he had to repeatedly douse flames that were between him and Dion. The water never made it to Dion. After a few minutes the two firefighters at the hole where Dion was trapped attempted to pull him from an enlarged opening, but found it was still too small. The fire was spreading so rapidly that they were almost caught in the same flames that suddenly engulfed Dion as the house collapsed further around him.

We are very grateful that these folks were courageous enough to try to rescue Dion and that he did not spend his last moments alone. From discussions with other neighbors since then, I have learned that many of the Richmond Hill residents, particularly those who were extremely close to the blast, had been in shock and had had difficulty getting even themselves out—and that the emergency responders were working to evacuate the area quickly.

The funeral was the day after the visitation. Hundreds of people attended, including prominent officials. I still felt dead inside, and did not care much who was there. The service was conducted by two ministers. One was my friend Bill Schwein, and the other was Monsignor Tony Volz.

On the day of the funeral, the city announced that the investigation had officially become a homicide investigation. We had suspected foul play, but had hoped it was not so. Then, just before Christmas, the first three people were arrested in the case and charged with murder, arson, and other crimes.

With the initial holiday season over, and three people in jail, we were faced with settling estates and determining the values of losses for the insurance company. This process was both prolonged and painful. Many memories returned, and the anguish of losing Dion and Jennifer overcame us frequently.

About two months after the explosion, our families were finally allowed to go into the site. Much had, by then, been hauled away as evidence or destroyed by the digging and investigating; but we were allowed to comb through what remained, to see if there was anything salvageable. Both Dion and Jennifer had collected things, and had memorabilia from early childhood. We found a few items of their collection of Muppet figures—some with damage and some almost perfect—a few photos, a single piece of china, a few tools, and a number of mangled and ruined items. There were remnants of gifts we had given them over the years. Jennifer's prized Indianapolis Colts brick was found in the area where Dion had died. No signs were ever found of their dog, Pepper.

Twenty months after the explosion, I found a magazine for Dion's CD changer sticking out of the ground where the basement had since been filled in. Except for some soil caked on the magazine, it appeared to be in good condition. I learned that the last CD Dion had purchased was by Van Morrison, who is one of my favorite musicians.

Dion and I shared so many interests, including a love of music, electronics, automobiles, running, family ... and flowers. The summer following the explosion, Dion's yard was covered with his flowers. His garden had been scattered, by the digging and sorting of debris, all across the yard and into the yard of the house that had exploded. We were able to recover many of the flowers and I planted most of them in my yard. In spite of considerable excavation of the yard, many more flowers emerged for us to retrieve during the second summer. Dion's flowers remind me of his determination and persistence.

This grief has been the greatest I have ever known.

Until this tragedy occurred, I had never realized how often I think of my children. Dion was the life of our family and holiday celebrations, with everyone wondering what he had planned. Even when he was only three years old, we would sometimes gather around to listen to him tell a story at bedtime. I have lost a sibling, both parents, close friends, and many relatives. It seems that, in time, I healed from those losses. The loss of a child makes no sense and feels so unfair. I find myself fighting off fear of losing one of my daughters or one of the grandchildren. I have wonderful stepchildren, too, and the loss of one of them would also be devastating.

At the time of the explosion, I was working on a project as a team leader and found it impossible, for the next eight months, to function effectively in that role. The grief has lifted some, but it has remained impossible to return to where I was prior to the tragedy. It has remained difficult to concentrate. In work and in life. Thursdays are now very difficult. That was often the day of the week when Dion and I had lunch. Saturday nights at 11 are difficult, since the explosion occurred at that time.

Dion's and Jennifer's dedication to family and friends will be missed more than anything. They did their best to make gatherings special by coming up with special gifts and food for each individual. Dion enjoyed both his own family and Jennifer's family. He was a mentor to his nephew Tylor, and spent much time with Jennifer's younger brother Joe. Several of Dion's friends told me stories of how he had changed their lives. I discovered he had been more active in college than I had known. He had made many friends at IUPUI and they wanted to commemorate his life. Staff at IUPUI asked me if they could establish a scholarship in his name.

Both Dion and Jennifer were also dedicated to their work. Although he did not have money to invest, Dion felt as if he were one of the founders of Indy Audio Labs, a new company he was helping to start. Jennifer, a beloved teacher, was extraordinarily devoted to her students.

Both touched many lives. And in their fifteen-year relationship, their love grew stronger. After Dion died, I found that they had still been sending each other little love notes, via text messages, several times a day.

Dion's sister Brookley was just a year younger than Dion. They were very close and had depended upon each other for support all their lives, so this loss has been very difficult for her. Brookley gave birth to twins in 2014. One is a boy named Liam Dion. The other is a girl named Willa. Liam was the first of them to smile, and he smiles frequently, just as his Uncle Dion did. Dion's older sister, Emily, has some of the same feelings experienced by parents. She had always looked out for Dion when they were growing up, and had grown to appreciate Dion's love and his abilities. Our oldest grandchild, Tylor, seemed to see Dion as a big brother. Tylor was a senior in high school when Dion died, and the loss has deeply affected him. Tylor has videotapes that Dion happened to leave with him. I have yet to watch them.

It seems difficult for many people to understand the effects of the loss of a child. Most are willing to admit they do not understand, but some feel that after a few weeks or a few months, a parent should "get over it." After a year had passed, one minister told me that everybody has losses, but they get over them, so I needed to move along in the process. He recounted for me a long list of his losses. His children were not on that list. Such encounters make the loss even more difficult.

The Mornings with the Dads group has been great support for me. Those Dads have been where I have been. They get it. I will never forget my first meeting with one of the Dads. I felt I was going to either explode or implode with grief and anger. The father had lost his daughter in a tragedy a number of years earlier. He was able to tell Don Buxton (Jennifer's dad) and me stories that gave us hope and took the edge off the feelings of aloneness and anger that were so strong during the first six months or more. The love and care of the men in

Mornings with the Dads is a valuable blessing to me. They have been willing to share my grief and have lifted me when I have needed it. Some of the grief is relieved by meeting with people who know how I feel. The Dads group is a safe place to express myself and release the anger and frustration. It helps me as I recover and rebuild life a little at a time.

I am very grateful for friends and family who have been here for me. Our grandchildren's hopeful and energetic approach to life makes the future brighter whenever I am with them.

Just prior to publication of this book, thirty-three months after the explosion, the first of the conspirators has been sentenced, in St. Joseph County by a St. Joseph County judge, to life without parole. Many of the details mentioned here have only recently been disclosed through the testimony of neighbors, firefighters and others who were drawn into the tragedy of that night. Four more conspirators await either trial or sentencing. The second trial is planned for 2016 in Fort Wayne.

The fact remains that nothing can bring back Jennifer and Dion. In Leslie Weatherhead's *The Will Of God*, he teaches that, after a tragedy, one's task is to return to seeking fulfillment in life by following Jesus. For me, that will include building upon the memories from Dion and Jennifer throughout the rest of my life.

I find myself still looking for Dion and Jennifer, and even thinking I see them. It seems that one day a newborn just a few hours old was smiling at me; then, the next, he is trapped in a burning house. The memories come and go … and span from that first smile he gave to his mother and me … to the night we spent hoping Jennifer and Dion were not those reported to have been killed. Sometimes Dion is a newborn … sometimes he is sixteen, working on a stereo. A clerk may remind me of Jennifer at twenty-two years old.

My grandchildren and daughters bring memories of Dion and Jennifer. Yellow roses, sunflowers, coneflowers, and many other flowers remind me of them. My grandson Tylor, Dion's nephew, has Dion's mannerisms, particularly in the way he speaks. All of Brookley's children have features reminiscent of Dion. A big, red, happy dog reminds me of their dog, Pepper, and of them. Dion loved the Cincinnati Reds and anything Purdue. Both he and Jennifer were big Indianapolis Colts fans. More reminders everywhere I look. Yellow cars and trucks, Yats restaurant, any mention of the name Klipsch, Dr. Pepper or root beer, German chocolate cake or Boston cream pie, and raspberries. Dion was good at mimicking characters from TV and movies, such as Garth from *Wayne's World* and the Church Lady from *Saturday Night Live*. Sometimes he and Brookley, together, would get into an act of mimicking characters such as Beavis and Butthead and have all of us laughing.

Sometimes the memories deliver smiles, and sometimes tears. I find myself wishing I could have been there to save him. I wish I would have taken them both out for a late night. I wish I could have died in their place. Maybe if I had gone to their house that evening, we would have walked around to the north side and smelled gas while looking at flowers. I wish I had been given the opportunity to hold grandchildren from them. Every imaginable "what if" scenario has passed through my mind. None of it does any good. Nothing will bring them back to us.

John Longworth

Samuel Xavier Motsay

June 26, 1997 – May 11, 2014

At the outset, I must say that I'm Sam's stepfather and, although he was not my biological son, I can't imagine I could have loved him more. I came into his life in May, 2003, when he was five, just before his birthday that coming June 26. My birthday happens to be June 28, which I will now associate with Sam's, and his passing, for the rest of my life.

Sam was very intelligent and a great student. He was also athletic and had natural basketball talent and skills.

When he was very young, he tried other sports, such as baseball and football. He enjoyed watching these sports, but not so much playing them. He then tried intramural league basketball, early in grade school, and was hooked. His great joy in life, other than basketball, was playing video games. He was good at them, too. He'd spend hours on end playing into the wee hours of the morning. We literally had to make him stop a lot of the time. Most of all, he loved to have fun.

When Sam was seven and his brother, Nick, was six, we took them to an all-inclusive resort hotel called the Barceló, in Ixtapa, Mexico. It has a beautiful beach with perfect waves for body surfing. We had great fun doing so. On the last day of our trip, Sam and I went down to the beach for one last swim and we saw a stingray jump out of the water—fly several yards in the air—and land back into a wave. In third grade, Sam drew a picture of his beach experience, along with a brief essay where he expressed it was like spending time in "paradise." Memories like these are now priceless and we're grateful we seized such opportunities for Sam to have grand and joyful experiences in his young life.

And no discussion about Sam can take place without saying *he knew what he wanted.* He'd decide he needed a new video game or pair of basketball shoes, a new computer—or whatever he fancied at the time—and he'd figure out a way to earn it. In retrospect, I'm glad we were kind and generous with him, within reason, and had the means to provide what he asked for, as his time was cut far too short.

When Sam was a freshman in high school, he had an assignment to choose a local professional in the type of career he might like to pursue, job-shadow that person for a day, and give a presentation on it to his class. A few years earlier, he had asked me what I did as a financial advisor and I had told him, in particular about managing investments for my clients. He had listened very intently and responded, "I see." Needless to say, it was my profession he chose to job-shadow. As he went through our offices and learned about financial planning, interacting with clients and the markets, I'd never in my life seen him more attentive and engaged in anything outside of school studies, sports or gaming. From this he expressed a serious interest in pursuing a career as a financial advisor. Well, I was excited about it and began planning to make an extra push to grow my practice by the time he graduated from college—to give him a start in the business, with a client base from which he could grow his own practice and eventually take over my business when I retired. I enthusiastically spent time thinking about teaching him the business, about how to interact with clients, and about the stock and bond markets. This was the future I was expecting to have with Sam. Now that future is gone and we will never have those experiences.

For years, Sam played basketball on various teams at Center Grove schools in Greenwood, Indiana, a south suburb of Indianapolis. He started playing on teams early in grade school, up to making the junior varsity team when he was a sophomore.

Some of the student athletes at Center Grove experiment with and use drugs, like some kids at most schools. In an effort to prevent student drug use, Center Grove School Corporation has implemented a random drug-testing program, which we as parents and students agree to by signing a consent form when students are freshmen, allowing the school to test students. I had mistakenly believed Center Grove School Corporation's random drug-testing program would identify any drug kids commonly use these days. I found out the hard way, they do not. The critical mistake schools make with their drug-testing programs is that students can identify which drugs they test for—and which drugs they do not. Students can also research how long various drugs stay in their system, to identify which drugs have a "short life" before they will no longer be detected in their urine. For example, based on the studies I've seen, which were verified by the Johnson County Sheriff's Office, the detection period for drugs such as lysergic acid diethylamide (LSD) and cocaine is less than one day. For this reason, LSD is not usually found on a five-, ten-, or even twelve-panel drug test.

Rumors occurred indicating that athletes at Center Grove High School had used drugs and successfully passed the random drug test. Sam had evidently decided to experiment with drugs, too, and was influenced to take hallucinogens, in particular, to avoid the school's drug detection tests. This came as a real shock, as Sam was always concerned about impurities, poisons and various bacteria and viruses getting into his body. He had been eating healthier foods in the months before he died, for this reason. It never occurred to us that he would ever consider experimenting with drugs, given the caution he always expressed about his body and overall health.

Saturday, May 10, 2014, was the day before Sam passed away. It was a weekend much like any other in the life of a dedicated young athlete. Sam was playing basketball on yet another Amateur Athletic Union (AAU) team to keep his skills sharp year-round in preparation for trying out for the Center Grove varsity team in the fall of 2014. He had two basketball games that day at Carmel High School, in a north suburb of Indianapolis. Jeanine had run him up there for a day-game where she took pictures and video-recorded him playing, as she had routinely done, with her iPhone. Afterwards, they bought some plants for our front porch and ran other errands to pass the time, as Sam had another late game that night.

That afternoon, we decided to grill steaks for dinner. Sam and I went to Meijer to get charcoal, as we had run out. When we got there, he picked up a twelve-pack of Baja Blast, a specialty soda he loved. Mountain Dew makes it for Taco Bell and it happened to be packaged for retail, for a limited time. We then picked up a bag of charcoal. On the way home, Sam expressed he was now eager to get his driver's license, which was a welcome change from the lack of urgency he'd had on the matter. That afternoon, I cooked Sam's last meal, which he finished. This was notable, as he was a picky eater and didn't always clean his plate.

The reason I mention these everyday events and family interactions is, at the time, we had no idea that would be the last day Sam would be alive. From time to time, we all hear the prophetic advice to value every day as though it may be our last. Well, it was for Sam—and for us, with him—and I now recognize the truth and value of that perspective.

That night, Jeanine and I drove Sam to his late game at Carmel High School ... again, not knowing that it would be the last time he would play a game of basketball. Afterwards, we stopped at a McDonald's to get him a snack and something to drink. When we got home, Sam said he was going to take a shower and go to a friend's house in our neighborhood. He planned to stay the night and would be back the next morning. It was good to hear he was spending time with a friend who was popular at school, rather than playing video games all night. He took a shower and left on his scooter just after 10:00 p.m. He returned briefly with his friends (there were now three of them), and said, "Ed, I need to get a charger," for his gaming controller. He went upstairs, then left again. Jeanine and I were sitting together in the family room when he walked out the door. That was the last time Sam would speak to me or we would ever see him.

Sam and his friends evidently had planned to take LSD that night, have a good time, and get back home to their respective families for Mother's Day the next morning. Instead the boys had been sold a new synthetic hallucinogen known as 25i-NBOMe or "N-Bomb." They each took two doses or blotter "tabs"—and Sam never woke up.

The next morning, on May 11—Mother's Day—I woke first, at around 9:00 a.m., and went downstairs to make coffee. Jeanine got up shortly after and joined me in the kitchen. We were talking about what we were going to do that day, when we heard the doorbell ring. We had two boys with friends in the neighborhood, so we didn't think much of it. I answered the door and there were two men standing on our front porch with somber looks in their eyes. It was Doug Cox, the sheriff of Johnson County, and Dan Meagher, a deputy coroner. I noticed the deputy coroner had Sam's ID in his hand, on top of a black leather-bound notepad he was carrying. Sheriff Cox then said that three boys had spent the night in a house in our neighborhood, had taken what appeared to be two doses of LSD, each, and that one of the boys did not show any signs of life—and had been deceased too long for any revival efforts to be effective. They needed one of us to identify the deceased young man in a photo they had taken on an iPad. I had started to go into shock. I was standing closest to the two men and, given the nature of the request, I was the better choice to identify "the young man." I looked at the picture, and it was indeed Sam. For the rest of my life, I'll never forget Sam's image in that photo. Sam's younger brother, Nick—who had been upstairs sleeping—had woken up, overhearing our interactions with the two men. He came downstairs only to discover his older brother had died the night before.

Sheriff Cox and Deputy Coroner Meagher stayed with us that morning until our pastor, Dave Schreiber of Resurrection Lutheran Church, arrived to support us. I asked to look at the photo a couple more times while the sheriff and deputy coroner were still at our home, hoping against hope I was mistaken and that the boy in the photo was someone other than Sam. Alas, it was not. As Pastor Dave was leaving a service which was in progress, to rush to our home, Pastor Mitch Phillips happened to be preaching to the congregation the prophetic words of David, from Psalm 23: "And though I walk through the valley of the shadow of death, I will fear no evil, for thou art with me, thy rod and thy staff, they comfort me." Jeanine also called her parents, who raced to our house from Danville, Illinois; and Sam's father, Francis Motsay, who drove down from Grand Rapids, Michigan.

It's impossible to express the state of shock, the level of grief, and how numb parents feel when they realize they've lost a child.

The worst day of our lives was then followed by the worst week of our lives. In spite of the state of unbearable grief we were in, we met with a representative at a funeral home near our neighborhood and made the visitation and cremation arrangements. Selecting a casket for the visitation, and an urn for Sam's ashes, was unreal to me. I recall sitting there, numb, almost in total denial of what was really happening. We met with Pastor Dave and other members of our church's staff to plan Sam's funeral and the meal afterwards. Jeanine and good friends of hers put together a video and memorial of photos of Sam for the visitation and service. I admire her strength doing so.

The visitation, held on Friday, May 17, was an experience. Again, Sam had been an outstanding student and athlete for years at Center Grove. He had impressed a lot of people and had made many friends along the way. His coaches and all the student basketball players at Center Grove came to extend their condolences and to give us a basketball they had signed commemorating his loss. For the next four-plus hours, Sam's teachers, school officials, and hundreds of students, friends and family came through.

The next day we held a funeral service for Sam at our church, followed by a buffet, for close friends and family. Pastor Dave did an outstanding job. In my opinion, it was the most uplifting funeral service I'd ever attended. In fact, one of Sam's former coaches said that it was the first time he'd ever left a funeral service feeling better than when he arrived. We did a balloon launch instead of a funeral procession of cars to a cemetery, as we had chosen to have Sam cremated rather than bury him. One of the attendees said they heard thunder in the distance just after we released some 200-plus balloons.

One critical element which occurred throughout the week after Sam died from taking 25i-NBOMe, and which has continued since then, is the media attention given to it. Sam was an honor student with a 4.038 grade point average on a 4-point scale, and an athlete. He was also nice looking and just sixteen years old. This was real news and it went on for weeks. We did not pay much attention to the media coverage the week Sam passed away, but we heard the stories:

repeated reports that Sam had overdosed on N-Bomb, accompanied by photos of the drug dealers.

The Johnson County sheriff's department, in concert with other law enforcement agencies in the Indianapolis area, did an exemplary job and apprehended the two drug dealers who had sold the drugs to the boys, as well as a drug kingpin on the north side of Indianapolis who had imported the drug into the country, likely from China, and created the blotter doses the boys took. The truth of the matter is, according to David E. Nichols, PhD—emeritus professor of pharmacology at Purdue University, and a leading expert on synthetic hallucinogens—NBOMe compounds are the most lethal psychedelics, that he's aware of, to hit the streets. To date, over twenty-five kids across the country have died from using the drug in ways they thought were safe, without knowing the purity or potency of the doses they were taking. Regrettably, I fear more kids will die from using NBOMe compounds going forward.

Since Sam's death, Jeanine has done several TV and radio interviews, and has spoken at numerous public forums, in an effort to educate students and the general public as to the dangers of 25i-NBOMe and other synthetic drugs, such as Spice—a synthetic form of marijuana which has also proven to be fatal to some users. Jeanine has also formed Sam's Watch, Inc., a 501(c)(3) non-profit organization, to get the word out about the dangers of synthetic drugs, in an effort to prevent young people from harming themselves, and to help save lives.

It has been just over eight months since Sam passed away, and the grieving continues. If you've lost a loved one, I'm sure you're aware of how overwhelming the grief can be. If you haven't, well, there's really no way to enable you to

121

understand, especially the loss of a child. Much has been written on the subject, such as the stages of grieving and what to expect. It really is a personal experience, as everyone grieves differently and at his or her own pace.

Initially, awareness of the finality of the loss caused the grief and shock to hit me like a tsunami. I was simply numb from it. I had no appetite, drank too much, and didn't get enough sleep. Needless to say, taking care of myself from the outset was important, but I had no motivation whatsoever to do so.

Grief counseling has definitely helped. Jeanine found an excellent grief support organization called Brooke's Place on the north side of Indianapolis. We met with our grief counselor, Donald Zimmerman, PhD—"Dr. Z"—as a family, and then individually. It is a holistic approach, as a big part of the grieving process is how we interact with and support each other. During one of my first meetings with Dr. Z, individually, I asked him how long the overwhelming initial shock and numbness lasts. He responded, "The *initial* overwhelming pain of the shock of a death, for many people, lasts five to six weeks. However, like all aspects of grieving, people grieve differently and there is no right or wrong in terms of how one grieves and how long it lasts." Anger and guilt were also a big part of the process for me—so much anger that Sam passed at such a young age, in the manner he did. Then there were the endless "what ifs" that ran through my mind, and guilt with regard to what I might have done to protect Sam and prevent his death. In the end I suspect, in most cases, the death of a loved one is simply out of our hands and beyond anyone's ability to control. Not that that changes the emotions we go through.

For me, it's been a matter of working through the grief. Dr. Z shared with me the following two quotes from a workshop he attended, given by Alan Wolfelt, PhD, one of the nation's leading experts on working with grief: "The only way to get to the other side is to go through it," and, "Sometimes you just need to sit in the belly of the whale." Both of these jewels of wisdom have to do with experiencing one's grief straight on and not avoiding it. This is the approach that seems to be working for me, although it's not easy. For some, medication works well and is clearly the necessary path. Reading, for me, is also essential. And there's no shortage of topics on the subject—from books like this one, written by parents who've lost children, to books and articles written by experienced counselors about healing from grief. Reading calms the mind, and is a way to better understand the grieving process—and to identify with the loss-experience shared by the author(s).

One of the first books Dr. Z recommended to me was *When Men Grieve: Why Men Grieve Differently & How You Can Help*, by Elizabeth Levang, PhD—with the following qualifier: "There are always exceptions to how men and women grieve, but in general, this book tends to be very helpful in understanding the differences." Essentially, men are socialized to be strong and manage their emotions and, consequently, deal with their grief largely in silence and alone. Women, on the other hand, are expressive about their feelings and actively seek to have conversations on their loss. An awareness of these differences is paramount, as grieving the loss of a child is often hard on marriages as well.

Very early on, my wife sought out and joined a couple of women's grief support groups, one of which is the "Moms" group—mothers who've each lost a child—and encouraged me to join the "Dads" group, which is largely composed of their husbands. It took me a while to do so, as I was dealing with a lot of anger, denial and guilt—and quite frankly, wasn't ready. Finally, I showed up one Thursday morning unannounced, introduced myself, and was welcomed with open arms. There were about ten fathers present that day. At the outset, everyone shared the story of the death of his own son and/or daughter. As I was sitting there looking around the table, listening, it occurred to me that, not only had all these men lost a child as well ... they truly *understood* what I was going through. I certainly had not had that experience before. Most people are either clumsy and don't know what to say, or say something inappropriate though well-meaning, if they say anything at all. Men do grieve differently, and to have a group of guys I can meet with is invaluable.

I joined the Dads group in October, 2014, and it has been instrumental in helping me in my grieving process. Sometimes we get together and merely chat about current events, sports, etc., and other times we talk about our losses and grieving. Most of the time, I go through the week keeping my emotions pent-up and guarded, and when I get to a Thursday morning meeting, the "wall" comes down and I experience my feelings around Sam's death in a safe environment, even if I don't say anything at all.

One of the fathers I met early on said to me, "Sorry to meet you," which is true. If Sam had not died, it is likely this Dad and I would have never met. That being said, for those of you who've lost a child, "sorry you are reading this book" ... and most of all, *so sorry for your loss*. I understand what you're going through. I wish you well in your grieving and encourage you to seek out and join a grief support group—or form one yourself, if necessary. It's a safe place to feel your loss and express your emotions with other men who "get it" and who will support you in a way others cannot.

In closing, I have two final items to share.

First, Sam's brother, Nick, is doing much better with grieving than his mother, Jeanine, and I. Most of the time he appears to be fine, although every now and then, I can see in his eyes he misses his older brother and is heartbroken they won't be growing old together.

And second, with regard to Sam, when he was in eighth grade, he affirmed his baptism via the rite of confirmation by making his public profession of faith to the congregation at our church. For Lutheran Christians, confirmation statements are based on a verse from the Bible, which each confirmand chooses. Sam chose John 14:2: "There are many rooms in my Father's home, and I'm going to prepare a place for you. If this were not true, I would tell you plainly." This verse is commonly associated with the death of a loved one and funerals. At the time, it seemed a bit unusual for Sam to base his confirmation statement on this Bible verse, but it was the one he wanted to use and he made it work quite well for his presentation. Sam's funeral service was held on Saturday, May 17. For liturgical Christians, John 14:2 was on the calendar to be the gospel reading the following day, May 18, the fifth Sunday of Easter. Pastor Dave eloquently mentioned Sam during his sermon, in relation to the Bible passage and his confirmation statement. Perhaps this was Sam's spiritual way of letting us know it was his time, and that he is now in the place Jesus prepared for him.

We love and miss you dearly, Sam. You are in our thoughts and prayers daily. And especially, thank you for reaching out from heaven. It's unmistakable, and comforting to know you are still with us in spirit, if not in body.

Ed Ochoa

Kathryn Michele Oxley
December 20, 1982 – October 9, 2007

"It was the best of days, and the worst of days!"

This is a well-recognized quote (slightly altered) from one of Charles Dickens' famous novels, *The Tale of Two Cities*. I use this quote because, as I reflect on that October day in 2007, it best describes how my day was lived by my family. As a Hoosier we complain about our weather as much as anybody in the country, but we will enjoy some of the most beautiful days. October 9, 2007, started as one of those fall days that blesses us with beauty that can come only from our creator! Mary, my wife of thirty-nine years, and our oldest daughter, Olivia, had decided to take our three grandchildren down to Brown County State Park for the day. A perfect 70-degree day, they let the kids ride the ponies and play in the playground area—and all dined on a wonderful picnic packed by Mary.

As the day was coming to an end, Mary received a call from Barry, whom our daughter Kate worked for in Florida as a waitress. Barry asked Mary if she had spoken with Kate, and informed her that Kate had not reported to work, had not called, and that there was no answer on her cell phone. Naturally, the anxiety was rising after the call. Mary and Olivia loaded the kids up and headed back towards Greenwood, making the almost fifty-mile trip toward home with a lot of uncertainty in their minds. Mary had called me on the trip down toward Brown County, and we had made plans to meet up with them for dinner upon their return to Greenwood, to finish a great day.

It had been a great day for me as well. Our fiscal year had just ended, and we were coming off of an exceptional year. I felt blessed to work with my son-in-law (Olivia's husband, Craig) as a partner in our wealth management practice that had had a record year. Along with the wealth management practice, I was the divisional director of the Heartland division, which was experiencing the fastest growth of the six divisions in Raymond James. I was enjoying the good weather and was looking forward to the family having dinner together that night. I was in Craig's office around 4 p.m., when I got paged by our receptionist that Olivia was on the phone for me. I stepped into our small conference room and, as I picked up the call, was expecting to confirm our dinner plans. I grabbed the phone receiver and answered with, "Hi Olivia"... and then my life began to change forever!!

Olivia shared the initial information they had gotten from Barry; she said that, since then, they had also learned that there were police and firefighters at Kate's apartment and that her apartment had been sealed off. Barry was headed over to try to get more information. I hung up the phone and felt totally numb as I walked past several desks and persons into my office, closing my door behind me. I fell into my chair, my body numb, my pulse racing. The clamminess of shock was setting in. As I was sitting at my desk, the door slowly opened. Craig stepped in and closed the door behind him. In a concerned voice he asked if I was okay. I looked at him, my eyes tear-filled, and told him that Kate hadn't been heard from since the previous night and that there were police and firefighters at her apartment complex with yellow tape around it. I told him I was going to his house so I would be there when Olivia, Mary and the kids arrived home. I picked my keys up and left the office in total silence, thinking the absolute worst and praying for a miracle from this nightmare.

On my way to their home, I stopped at a traffic light. As I sat there, Kate's life went through my mind. ... I see her as a little girl playing with her Barbies ... wearing her Michael Jordan jersey to the Pacer game ... her first time tasting the shrimp cocktail sauce at St. Elmo. The tears were running down my cheeks. I kept thinking that this had to be a nightmare that I would wake up from. The car behind me honked its horn and I realized I had missed the green light. As I continued driving, I became nauseous, not knowing how to face my wife, daughter, and grandkids, and be the strong leader of the family, as I was ready to become a total mess at any minute!!

... I arrive at Olivia and Craig's home as Mary and Olivia arrive with the kids. Mary comes immediately to my

129

arms and sheds tears, asking me what we will do without Kate. I try to show strength and state that we should think positively and wait till we have additional information. Mary, Olivia, and I sit at the kitchen table, discussing the known details and how it was left as far as when any additional information would be given to us. I call Barry to find out if he has learned anything more. As I dial his number it becomes harder with each digit. I do not want to hear the words that I fear are waiting for me. Barry answers, and as I identify myself, the phone becomes silent for what seems to be ten minutes, but are actually only a few seconds. He starts to talk. "It's bad Jim, it's the worst. I can't tell you how this hurts me." I thank him for all he has done and that we will talk later. I hang up. ... I slowly re-enter the kitchen area and feel the eyes of Mary and Olivia awaiting any news I have. I look up and slowly say that she's gone, our precious Kate is gone. The scene is etched in my brain: Olivia screams and falls to her knees, Mary and I fall into each other's arms, and Olivia rises and joins the hug. The next several hours we all sit in a state of disbelief, hoping that this will pass in the morning.

We were joined at that table that evening by our pastor, Tom; my sister, Ellen; my in-laws, Bill and Eleanor; and my sister- and brother-in-law, Jill and Rich.

It is said that family comforts at a time of need, and during this evening, I remember a solemn atmosphere with a caring and love. I made several calls to family and close friends and found it comforting to hear the care and love that many shared over the phone. The Bible speaks of "from the mouths of babes" and, as Mary was crying, our oldest granddaughter went over to her, looked up at her, and said, "Maime, you shouldn't be crying, because Aunt Kate is in heaven now."

That first evening moved in slow motion … sitting around the kitchen table, the Greenwood police coming to the house to give the official word from the Clearwater, Florida, police of Kate's passing … the officer, a young man who had been in school with both Olivia and Kate at Greenwood High School. As the evening came to an end, Mary and I went home, emotionally tired and erased of much of our energy. It is still taking hold in my thought. *My sweet daughter has died in an apartment fire.* She was only twenty-four and had so much ahead of her. She loved her family so much!!! The hurting is quickly setting in and I am realizing the fact that this is going to be hard—and I'm not sure I'm equipped to be a grieving father!

I woke early the next morning and grabbed the newspaper. It is our local paper and carries mostly the local events and stories, with outside news appearing a day or two later. So, to my surprise, as I slowly turned the pages, there it was … the headline confirming what I was still hoping was a nightmare I'd wake from. *Former resident dies in apartment fire.* Reading the article, it resonated with me that this feeling, the nauseous hurting feeling, was going to be with me for a long time!!

I wasn't aware that this was the grieving process starting.

Kate's life celebration was a comforting experience. Friday night's visitation was a long evening; however, there were friends of Kate's and ours who had travelled from far to be there. That was unexpected and heartwarming. The morning of her service was surreal as Mary and I got dressed. I was hoping to wear a tie that Kate had given me, but I had tried before and it had been too short. Today, amazingly, it fit like a tie should!! As I was driving to the church, I was praying that this service would be blessed, and that Olivia would have peace as she gave the eulogy for her sister. I had wondered, when she first mentioned that she would give the eulogy, how she would be able to get through it the day of the service. I knew that with His grace, she would!! As we arrived, we walked to the church hand in hand. It was a place that had been our church home for so many years. Our families had witnessed baptisms here for my wife and our two daughters; weddings for Mary and me, my brother- and sister-in-law, and Olivia and Craig; and now we were here to celebrate the life of our beautiful twenty-four-year-old daughter, Kate. I had so many questions and feelings all being bottled up so that I could get through the celebration without breaking down too much!!

As our church began to fill, many individuals approached me with condolences and love. The music and slide show oftentimes caught my attention and froze my movement with memories of Kate's life and many good times, leading to a heavy heart and teary eyes. The pews continued to fill, and as we approached the service time, I looked toward the front of the church and there stood a very dear longtime friend, Kent, who had driven in from South Carolina. SO touching to have friendship this deep!! The service was such a celebration. Olivia's eulogy was so heartfelt. The scripture readings, the message and music—all still are engraved on my heart. We had a family dinner with some invited friends at our club … with continued sharing. As everyone left and headed their separate ways, Mary and I were exhausted but felt blessed from all of those who had travelled to support us through this difficult loss of Kate.

This is when reality sets in, when the rubber meets the road: when all those who, during the past week, have been calling, visiting, bringing food, sending cards … are gone.

They have returned to their normal lives. I wake up and realize that my normal has been changed forever. I look around and don't understand normal anymore. Grieving has begun, but how long will it last? When will it be over? How do I deal with it? ... I wanted a manual. I didn't want to take too much time to grieve publicly. However, I quickly found out that grief was not a process that could be controlled, and that it must be allowed to go fully *through* its process for each one of us!

Early on I handled this process poorly, mainly because I was trying to handle it. I wanted to mourn on my schedule—on demand—and be able to shut it off when I wanted to. After about six to nine months, it became apparent that my life was being affected by my style. During this period, when I thought I was handling it, I found myself working longer days than normal; crying while driving to locations; forcing myself to act like I was present during meetings; and staying in my hotel, drinking a fifth of Jack Daniels by myself—behavior all of which was out of character for me. However, when these patterns first appeared, I didn't worry about them. I kept pushing my schedule, thinking I could suppress my grief and not deal with it—a response probably typical for a lot of men, and some women, who are not wanting to face the reality of the loss of a dear one.

For me, this was the most difficult step in the grieving process. Truly accepting the loss and dealing with it honestly. Facing the fact that Kate was not going to call me, or come home, or ask me to get her tickets to a concert. I was not going to hold her little girl clammy hands again. Not until we were together again in heaven!

I needed to allow the grieving process to work through me, but had felt I needed to be strong for Mary and

Olivia. Mary, who was suffering the loss of her daughter; and Olivia, who was dealing with the loss of her only sibling. Her sister. Olivia shared during this time, that people would often ask how Mom and Dad were doing, but seldom asked how *she* was doing.

Through this grieving process, we have become much more aware of those around us who have losses. There are learning opportunities even in the midst of grief, if we are open to growing and don't let bitterness prevent this from happening. I am sure many of us have seen the further damage that anger and bitterness can inflict. This bitterness, if allowed, will strip any joy or happiness that may ever return. It inhibits the healing that might happen otherwise, and stifles our ability to openly remember our loved one with love and tell those stories we have of them.

Kate left certain things that are engraved on our hearts forever, that whenever they are talked about among friends … or when a particular song is heard … or when our grandchildren talk about their Aunt Kate … it makes her so real to me and I can rejoice in her life. At times, that rejoicing is through smiles, and other times through tears. But always with loving memories.

I am not sure how many times I've heard, "you will get through this," and, "it gets a lot easier." I was told by so many that "she is in a better place" … and my beliefs are assured with that promise of eternal life. But, as her earthly father, her best place is here for me to watch after her.

The grieving process is difficult and complex— different for everyone, but the same for everyone!! It consists of separation, depression, pain, acceptance, and trying to learn to live life with a "new" normal. I've had counseling, and almost eight years later, I still need antidepressants to help me cope with life's challenges. All of those challenges are not from Kate's passing—but losing her forced me to face a lot, which has caused me to totally reassess my life. Today I am a better person because of having gone through all of these steps. I am much more compassionate; my relationship with Christ is much closer; my priorities have changed. Kate's passing was devastating in so many ways and has left scars. But the aftermath has brought some good.

I don't think grieving ever really ends.... IT GOES FOREVER, FOREVER. Approaching eight years since Kate's passing, I would say that the grieving has largely passed. However, some remains and I would never want what is left, to end. For me, this remaining portion of hurt shows me that the love is enduring this separation. There are still times I have tear-stained cheeks for no apparent reason. At times my heart seems that it is going to explode from pain, and I just wish I could visit with her for a day.

To see my precious Kate is something I forever long for. And then I remember we are separated, but only temporarily, until we rejoin in heaven. Life continues to move on, here, and I need to be a participant in this life.

And, I know Kate is cheering me!!

Jim Oxley

Steven Henry Pawlik &
Katrina "Katie" Lynn Pawlik

THEN THERE WAS ONE

It was the best of times, it is the worst of times, it was the age of joy, and it is the age of tragedy. This is the story of the loss of two of three children. Gone are a son and a daughter. Katie died eight years and two days after Steve's death. One struck suddenly by accident, the other taken by illness. Both deeply loved. Both profoundly missed.

> *... It is tough being the only child....*
> —Michael Pawlik, February 4, 2014

This is also about lessons learned of how to deal with the losses, grief and survival from a generation where "real men don't cry" ... and about how having a cup of coffee with a group of fathers can make it all better.

> *It is indeed a much greater thing that I do now*
> *than I have ever done.*
> —Charles Dickens, *A Tale of Two Cities*

Steven Henry Pawlik
July 9, 1970 – February 2, 2006

My wife, Pat, and I were living in Gainsville, Virginia, while I completed my four-year tour in the army. Steve was born on July 9, 1970, in Manassas, Virginia. I was hoping he would be born on the Fourth of July so I could name him Patrick Henry after his mom (Pat) and his dad (Henry). My wife prayed every day of the pregnancy that he would be born on any day other than the 4th. She won.

I had been raised, without siblings, by my grandparents and then an aunt and uncle who were up in their years. I was not familiar with infants, toddlers and the likes.

When we had Steven, I remembered all our friends who had constantly complained about their children's behavior. I couldn't understand what they were talking about. But I would discover that Steve was an exceptionally good-natured and well-behaved child; and as life went on, and we had more children—expanding our household range of personality and expression—I began to empathize with my friends' plight.

By 1973 we had moved from Virginia back home to Indiana and then on to the Chicago area. While in Indiana, we were blessed with our second son, Michael. Steve and Michael truly loved and enjoyed each other from the minute Mike was born till Steve passed. Ten years after Steve, and seven years after Mike, we were blessed with a "Catholic surprise": our daughter, Katie. (Her story follows.)

Steve was a bright and gifted child who never struggled with any academic challenges. I sent him to a strict all-boy Catholic high school. The US Marine Corps could not have run the school any more strictly than the Marist Brothers. Steve's success in high school allowed for his choice of colleges, including an academic scholarship from the University of Miami ("The U"). I remember asking why he chose The U over Michigan or Northwestern. His answer was simple, but insightful: "If you had to go to school in winter, where would you go?"

Steve really enjoyed Miami. He lived in Coral Gables and partied in South Beach. He once asked me how I knew where he partied. It was easy. I told him I was buying the Clevelander one American Express bill at a time.

By this time Steve was an avid Grateful Dead fan (Dead Head). One summer, he came home from Miami and I asked him what he was going to do while he was home. He told me he was going to try to "find himself." I had no idea what that meant. So I strongly urged him to "find himself" a job. And I helped him. A friend of mine gave him a job unloading quarter sides of beef from 2 a.m. to 10 a.m. during his summer break. The quarters of beef probably weighed as much or more than he did. At the time, he hated every minute of it—but, before going back to school, he thanked me for the lessons learned. He realized his coworkers would be there the rest of their lives and he was getting an education and the chance at a better future.

After graduation, Steve went to work for various major brokerage houses and, in 1995, we decided we would move to Las Vegas together. We had no idea what fate awaited us.

Michael and our old Chicago friends would visit frequently. When you live in Vegas, you are never short of visitors. Katie joined us after she graduated from high school. She and I really enjoyed Vegas together. We were fond of the shows, food and action Vegas had to offer, and also traveled from there to Mexico and Hollywood.

After three years, Steve left to work for a large San Francisco brokerage house, and that same year Katie returned to Chicago. Now that I look back over those years, I realize the time the three of us had together was a precious gift. I've lost two of my children, but I haven't lost the memories of them.

After a couple of years in the Bay Area, Steve, preferring the Las Vegas life to the San Francisco life, returned. We were baseball fanatics who really enjoyed going to spring training in Arizona and major league games in San Diego, Los Angeles and Phoenix. We were making the most of the Vegas experience.

Steve was full of life. To meet him was to love him. He had an aura that brought out the best in people. His radiating and optimistic personality made a friend of everyone he had ever met.

All his zest, all his kindness. Wiped out in the blink of an eye.

February 2, 2006, was a typical Vegas winter day. The sun was shining and the temperature was in the 50s. Steve was driving south on I-15, the main corridor through Las Vegas, no doubt enjoying the sun and beautiful Nevada scenery. Suddenly his car was starting to have mechanical problems. He pulls onto the brim of the highway, gets out of the car and lifts the hood. He puts the hood back down and walks around the front of the car, not concentrating on where he is at—and steps into an I-15 travel lane. He is struck by a car. A family on vacation going to Disneyland. The Nevada state police calculated the speed in excess of 70 miles per hour.

The details were in the police report. I also requested a copy of the autopsy. If there is one lesson I wish I could convey to everyone, it is *never read an autopsy report*. The nightmare is with me forever. Steve died quickly, painlessly, and his place in heaven was reserved for him. He was a deeply religious and practicing Catholic. That says a lot about a young man in his thirties living in Sin City.

From the moment I received the news of Steve's death, I immediately thought, "There is nothing on God's earth could ever equal such a personal tragedy." I was wrong.

Not knowing how he lost himself, or how he recovered himself, he may never feel certain of not losing himself again.

—Charles Dickens, *A Tale of Two Cities*

141

Katrina "Katie" Lynn Pawlik

January 25, 1980 – February 4, 2014

Katie was born January 25, 1980. That was the beginning of a life filled with what seemed to be insurmountable challenges. Just days after her birth, I took her to our pediatrician for her first checkup. The doctor immediately noticed a problem. Both legs were out of the hip sockets. In order to correct this condition, she was required to stay in the hospital, for months, in traction. Traction is not easy on a newborn baby. After the hospital stay, she was in a full body cast for a year. That was only the beginning.

A daughter has a special place in a father's heart, especially when she is the only girl and a late "surprise." Watching her live in a body cast for a year strengthened our relationship even more. This precious little girl would need my help more than I could ever imagine.

Very early in Katie's life, we started to notice her unusual behavior. She was diagnosed with bipolar disorder. That is a heavy cross for anyone to carry, especially a child. She would fight those demons her entire life. Being the youngest of three, she also had a real independent streak. She would need every bit of it. Kids can be really cruel to other kids who are not like them. As she was growing up I became more and more protective of her, and her mother and I were determined to make her life as happy as possible.

Katie's goal was to join Steve and me in Vegas when she turned eighteen. She and I had a deal: she wanted to come to Las Vegas—and I wanted her to prove the world wrong by graduating from high school. We both lived up to the deal. She really enjoyed Vegas, but returned home to her mother after she became pregnant.

Some combination of medicine, prayer and hope helped to control the bipolar disorder in her later years.

So much in life is judged by status or material accumulations, and not by the most important needs of society. Katie was a role model, not a supermodel. There is no more sacred duty than motherhood, and Katie proved to be an exceptional mother. As Steve had mentioned during his college years a desire to find himself, Katie found herself when she became a mother. She raised three beautiful children—Alyssa, Morgan and Logan—whom she loved deeply. The life of a single mother of three is a daily struggle, but Katie did it with grace, perseverance and strength.

Katie had struggled most of her entire life, from the moment she was born, and had finally reached normalcy and joy.

And then it was suddenly gone.

After Steve's death, I had returned to Indiana and moved in with Michael and his family. During this time, my relationship with Katie grew closer and closer. The "princess" had come of age. Daddy's little girl had become a lady and mother. And the tide began turning. Now the daughter is becoming the protector of the aging father. She called me four or five times a day to check on me. It drove me absolutely crazy.

Now Katie is gone forever. The phone never rings and the silence is deafening.

Katie died February 4, 2014, from complications of pneumonia. In death, as in life, she gave of herself to others. There are many organ recipients living a much better life because of my Katie.

... you are lost dream of my soul ...
—Charles Dickens, *A Tale of Two Cities*

The Shock Effect

There is a common thread that runs through the great majority of Dads in our group. It is the suddenness of the death of the child. Most died by either violence, accident, suicide or sudden fatal medical ailment. What does the group have that appeals to these fathers? Having lost a son suddenly to an accident and a daughter to illness, I have an insight as to the answer to the question. This is not meant to imply that the sudden loss is any more or less a tragedy than a loss for ongoing medical reasons. Any loss of any child is an excruciating loss. I call what draws the Dads together "the shock effect." It stuns and paralyzes even those of us—which are the majority in the group—whose "children" were adults when they passed. We know we've had more time than many parents get, and are so grateful for the time we've had; but the history with that child is that much deeper, and the dreams for their future are no less full of hope and expectation.

Even as parents of adult children, our cycle of parenthood has been cut short of its full fruition. From the time we discovered we were having a child, we planned our and the baby's future. Life is wonderful. Love is everywhere. Then, the child has grown up. The tough job of raising him, or her, is over. Now is the time to enjoy them as they move into adulthood. They are off to college or work and making their way in the world. Mom and Dad are proud of the successes they have created. Hopefully sometime in the future there will be grandchildren. The future will continue to get better and better.

Suddenly the phone rings or there is a knock at the door. Life as we know it, is over. The future is lost. We are helplessly lost in a fog of grief. The child we've guided and protected from the perils of life is—gone. Dead. All the years of love, nurturing and devotion are erased. There was no time for preparation. There was no final "I love you." No opportunity for "I'll do whatever it takes." Just finality.

The instantaneous death leaves a hole in our heart that will last forever. Nothing we can do will ever replace the lost opportunity of saying "good bye." The raw feelings become unbearable. The emptiness in our soul will be a cross to bear the rest of our life. This is a facet of a child's death that no one can comprehend unless they experience it. I look around the room at every meeting, thinking *these men know and understand*. That is why we are here. We will grieve forever while bearing the shock effect, together.

Tell the wind and the fire where to stop; not me!
—Charles Dickens, *A Tale of Two Cities*

A Herd of Elephants Becomes a Group of Dads

What I say next will surprise no one: men and women grieve differently. And those around them respond differently to each.

Sympathy, understanding and compassion are felt for both in a time of loss, but the father and mother do not pass through the experience of the loss in the same way. Nor are they regarded in the same manner.

Everyone understands the mother. They *know* she is devastated. She is showered by grieving mourners, family and friends. She has a circle of support she will reach out to—and who will reach out to her.

Now let's go see the father. Dad is who we affectionately call the "elephant in the room." Do I really have to say anything to him? What do I say? Here is how it usually goes: "Sorry about your loss. How do you think the Cubs are going to do this year? Nice to see you again. Bye."

Fathers are stoic. All through history we know that "real men don't cry." Everyone deals with grief in his or her own way. But there are certain attributes that are common to all—even men, and especially dads who've lost a child: it is necessary to talk about feelings and release them. We all harbor grief, hate and emptiness. That leads us to two important questions. What do we do about these feelings? (The answer is unique to everyone.) Even more important is, Where can we do it?

The group.

The group is NOT a twelve-step program, prayer meeting or bereavement class. We are a group of dads who have walked the walk and talked the talk of both parenthood and loss. Our slogan is "We get it." No textbooks or charts on how to grieve. Just real life experiences. We find our support comes from talking to one another. We talk sports, news, politics. A group of guys having a cup of coffee. We often socialize by going out to ball games, restaurants, and fundraisers. We discuss our kids, but we do not feel compelled to dwell on grief. We know, all too painfully, what has brought us together. We are here to help one another along a journey of grief, and when we share our passions with others, our lives start to feel better.

To other grieving fathers, we say, Why don't you give us a try? You will never be a stranger. We get it.

I've lost two of three children. Immeasurable tragedies. Most of the strength to deal with the second death came from this group of Dads. It is so comforting to be able to lean on cohorts who understand and care. They "get it."

A wonderful fact to reflect upon,
that every human creature is constituted to be that
profound secret and mystery to every other.

—Charles Dickens, *A Tale of Two Cities*

Henry Pawlik

Christopher Michael Rhoads
November 19, 1967 – June 20, 2008

June 20, 2008, was a Friday evening that changed the dynamics of our family forever.

My wife, Michele, and I were in Greenwood, Indiana, spending the evening with our friends Charlie and Wanda. Wanda had just found out her cancer had come back, and we were visiting them, eating pizza, and trying to cheer her up. Wanda had been in remission twice before, and we were all certain she would beat this again.

Around 7 p.m., Michele's cell phone rang. It was our youngest son Dustin's girlfriend, Tami, calling hysterically about Christopher, our middle son. She said he was sweating profusely and could not cool down. Michele told her to put Chris on the phone so she could ask him some questions to see how alert he was. She asked him his name—and why he wasn't letting Tami call 911. He kept saying, "I'll be alright, I just need to cool down and lay down." As a child, whenever Chris was sick, all he wanted to do was go to bed and sleep. He thought that would cure any ailment he had. Michele told Chris to put Tami back on the phone, and she told Tami to dial 911 immediately.

When Michele's cell phone rang again, a few minutes later, it was Dustin calling—saying that Chris was dead.

We left Charlie and Wanda's immediately after Dustin's call, arriving at Chris's home in about twenty minutes. I do not remember driving there, because I was trying to console Michele, and I am sure I was also numb and in shock. It seemed surreal, like a dream, and I kept hoping I would wake up, and that Chris would wake up also.

We would find out that Christopher had worked all day, and had even stopped at the Beech Grove American Legion Post to have one drink. He had felt dizzy and was asked if he needed help getting home, but of course he refused. When he got home, his condition didn't improve, and when Dustin and Tami dropped by, he asked Dustin to go get Angie from work at the Salvation Army. So, Dustin left to pick up Angie, Christopher's fiancée. That's when his condition went from bad to worse. Chris passed out while Tami was calling 911. She tried to resuscitate him with mouth-to-mouth CPR until the EMTs arrived. The EMTs arrived within ten minutes of Tami's call, but could not revive him.

Chris died on a Friday evening and I went back to work on Monday because I thought I had to in order not to completely lose my mind. Fortunately, a good friend and boss sent me home to take care of the arrangements for our son. I put on my "strong" face and took charge for my wife and family, coordinating communications with Chris's children, his ex-wives, and other family members on my side and Michele's. I merely packed my emotions away and dealt with this as a new challenge that I could overcome and conquer. There was no time to mourn or break down emotionally—even at the funeral home, when we had one last time to see him before he was cremated. I had to keep it together for Michele, our sons, and our grandchildren.

Almost a year and a half earlier, in February of 2007, my mother had died and was cremated. After the service, Michele and I wanted to tell our sons what arrangements we would like, so they would not be stressed out with making all of those decisions quickly and under emotional duress. All three sons voluntarily told us what they would like, as well. Little did we know that sixteen months later, we would be fulfilling the wishes of one of them.

The week following Chris's death was a blur with phone calls and arrangements to get everyone to our house prior to the viewing and service. He left behind three teenagers when he died: Ryan, Brittany, and Isaac. We drove down to French Lick for his oldest son, Ryan, and picked up Brittany and Isaac in Bloomington on the way back. Our oldest son, Parker, and his wife, three children and four grandchildren made the trip from Atlanta, Georgia. Dustin was living with us.

So we had a full house, and those days and nights were spent with memories and stories of Chris and his escapades. We concluded that Chris had crammed a lot of living in his short forty years on earth. He had been in the army, in Germany, when the Berlin Wall came down; and he had always been athletic … and that may have contributed to his premature death. He left lasting impressions on everyone he knew. An example of this was that his fiancée, two ex-wives, and three former girlfriends all attended his memorial service, and they were all amicable with each other.

Christopher was the type of person you wanted to spend time with. He always defended the underdog and would do just about anything for you if asked.

As I write this in August of 2015, over seven years later, I still cannot get the last image of my son out of my mind. It haunts me on my melancholy days when his absence is extremely painful. He is lying on the living room floor with his dog, Mona, nuzzling his arm, and his fiancée, Angie, kneeling beside him holding his hand, and he still has a trach tube in his mouth.

I try to picture him, instead, in my La-Z-Boy chair after we have had a family dinner and he is taking a nap. This is a much more positive image, but it doesn't always win out over the one in the aftermath of that Friday evening, at 7:50 p.m., when our forty-year-old son, Christopher Michael Rhoads, was pronounced dead of *natural* causes. Specifically, the death certificate said "myocardial infarction" as the immediate cause and "hypertension" as the underlying cause.

When my mother died, one month and one day shy of one hundred years, I could honestly say her death was of natural causes. She had had a good and long run! Our son did not, and died too soon—and it was *not natural*. I don't care how they classify his death. In my mind, *"natural"* is not what I would call it. If in fact his death was *natural*, then there should not be any "what ifs." But there are, and Michele and I both discuss these "what ifs" at times when our hearts are heavy or when we are having a bad day because we miss Chris.

Due to circumstances not germane to this chapter, Chris and Dustin graduated from high school together and it created a bond that was deep and lasting. When Christopher died, Dustin lost not only a brother, but also his best friend. To this day, no one has replaced Chris in Dusty's life. Dusty has since married and is now, at age forty-four, a stepfather and grandfather, but I can see there is still a void we all share. Parker misses Chris, too, and has relocated back to Indiana from Georgia, because he wants to be closer to family.

No one is unscathed by this tragedy in our family. We all have good days, and bad days, and rotten days. It is always there, just under the surface ... tsunamis suddenly appear without warning and without a cause. Then other times we can predict when we will have rotten days. Holidays, Chris's birthday, the date of his death are always difficult, even now, seven years later. It could be seventy years and it will still be difficult, because our family chemistry has changed and will never again be what it was.

I have a hard time explaining the family-chemistry component to someone who has not experienced it firsthand. It doesn't have to be a son or a daughter. It could be a grandparent or parent who passes away—and suddenly family traditions start dissolving because no one else wants to be in charge. Chris was the bonding element. When he died, Ryan, Brittany, and Isaac quit coming to see us. Parker and his family couldn't come up from Georgia for the holidays, because of finances and work schedules. Dustin, no longer with Tami, has since married Stacey and now lives with her. Instead of waking up on Christmas morning in our 1300-square-foot three-bedroom home with fifteen to nineteen people representing children, grandchildren, and great-grandchildren, we now wake up with our two cats and go out to eat breakfast with another couple.

Chris was the glue that kept our family together in a lot of ways. The last several years of his life, he worked for a company that toured the country introducing new products for the upcoming year. He was on tour with the crew that marketed new lines of tires, and was away from home eight to nine months every year. Consequently, he talked to his brothers quite frequently by phone and was the link between Parker and Dustin. Now that he is gone, they are having a difficult time reconnecting with each other. Chris would call his mother at least once or twice a week and she would tell me all about his current location and upcoming itinerary. We both miss those calls and the plans we'd make for family dinners upon his return. Now you know why I picture him taking a nap in my La-Z-Boy chair after a family dinner. ... We still have taco casserole for dinner, which was his favorite.

In addition to ongoing family traditions that we had with Chris, we have established a new tradition since Chris's death. Chris liked his Jack Daniels and he would chase it with a Mountain Dew or Pepsi. So, on his birthday, November 19, and on the date of his death, June 20, we have a shot of Jack Daniels in his honor. We had a shot of "Jack" on one other occasion: two years after his death, when his oldest son, Ryan, got married. At the reception, Ryan had Chris's immediate family members stand up and drink a shot in Chris's honor.

I've told you what we do each year on his birthday and the anniversary of his death, with shots of Jack Daniels. Let me fill you in on what else we have done to cope with this loss. Chris loved the ocean and our family trips to

Daytona Beach, Florida. So, in October, 2008, after his death (June, 2008), we all went to our time-share condo in Daytona and had a ceremony on the beach, and scattered some of his ashes in the ocean, in his memory.

The following June, 2009—on the first anniversary of Chris's passing—we wanted to do something special to honor him. Because Chris always had tattoos and would show us any new ones he had gotten commemorating his children or his dogs, Dustin got the idea to have a tattoo party at our house and have an original tattoo in memory of Chris inked on each of us: Parker, Dustin, Michele, and me. We had a tattoo artist from Crawfordsville, who was a friend of Dustin's, come to the house. He was someone Chris had known, too, and he had done some of Chris's tattoos. Dustin did a beautiful job of designing the tattoo, representing Chris and Chris's life. In Dustin's words, the three perpendicular steel bars represent the three brothers—and Chris, in particular, because he was strong like steel. The three horizontal steel bars—intertwined with the vertical bars, to form a cross, with white for depth and accent—represent his three children. His initials "CMR" fill a heart below the point where the bars cross. As Dustin says, no one put their heart into something, or loved, as sincerely as Chris. My tattoo also has "Son"—and Parker and Dusty have "Brother"—in a purple ribbon that drapes across the top, then down around the cross. Michele has only the heart, with his initials "CMR" in the heart, on her left shoulder blade. Chris had a big heart and it was his heart that took him from us. The tattoo party was a great time for all of us, and we each wear the tattoo proudly.

But even the shots of Jack and tattoo party didn't seem to be enough to take away the hurt and sadness if we let our emotions out. I had a particularly hard time accepting the fact that I needed to find a constructive way to deal with my emotions. When it weighed on me the hardest, I became moody, withdrawn, and non-communicative.

One day, my stepbrother Tom dropped off a book for me to read, titled *Tuesday Mornings with the Dads*. I was at work, so he gave the book to Michele and told her he had thought of me when a group of these Dads spoke at his church about how they were dealing with the loss of sons and daughters. How they were prompted to write their experiences to help other men who maybe need a positive way to deal with their own loss. Tom also told her there was a group on the south side that met on Thursday mornings at 7 a.m. at Bob Evans. I kept telling myself I was doing fine and didn't need someone telling me what I could do to feel better. Michele kept telling me I wasn't doing that well and it wouldn't hurt to at least read the book. I must have started and stopped four or five times before I finally got through two of the chapters the Dads had written. It was heart-breaking and yet therapeutic. It allowed me to cry—really cry, for our son who had left a huge void in our hearts and lives. I don't believe I had cried more than once or twice in the twenty-plus months since his death, until I started reading the Dads' stories. Over the course of the next several weeks, I promised myself I would finish the book and also attend the southside group of Dads at least once.

Due to my work schedule—which meant leaving the house by 7:15 a.m.—I was not able to attend the southside Dads group until late October, 2010, following my retirement October 1, 2010. I walked into the Bob Evans restaurant in Greenwood and didn't know a single person. All of the information I had was from the book and the northside Dads who had written the chapters. I have never been a shy introverted person—having made my living in the ministry, and in the corporate sales world—but I was a little nervous. They immediately welcomed me and took away all the anxiety I was feeling. I was told I didn't have to do or say anything. They all introduced themselves to me and told me their stories about their sons or daughters. I knew this was a safe place and that these men understood. I told them about our son Christopher and how he had died and how much we miss him.

That was four years and ten months ago when I walked into this group. Since then, I have missed only for medical reasons and trips; and even then I miss the fellowship, and my week is a little longer because of my absence. We have welcomed many new Dads to our group and I hope they feel the same as I do. The group serves a vital purpose of helping men deal with loss, in an environment with other men who have also experienced loss. You don't volunteer for this group, but you are glad it is there if you qualify.

As we pass the seventh anniversary of Chris's death, his cremains are still in our living room in a memorial, in our entertainment center. Michele does not want him anywhere else at the present time. My family and I will always miss Chris, whether it is seven years or seventy years, because we are less without him in our lives. My wife misses his mustache kisses. I miss his bear-like hugs. Our family members each miss him in their own special ways, because he spread so much laughter and love in his short years of life with us.

We love you, Chris!

Richard Rhoads

Peyton Ann Riekhof
March 6, 1995 – July 21, 2013

As I begin writing this chapter, I'm ten months into the worst year of my life. In some ways it feels like yesterday, and in other ways it seems like ten years ago. My mornings still bring feelings of disbelief and the constant asking of, "did this really happen?" … and then the day progresses to simply surviving … and trying to find some peace, and a little joy.

My life changed forever on July 18, 2013, around 3 a.m. This was the night we were awoken by a friend of our eighteen-year-old daughter, Peyton. This friend, Cody, had texted our older daughter, Jessy (nineteen), telling her to get us up and that he was coming over. He was concerned for

Peyton, who had been at his house that evening. This would be the start of three days of hell. We would soon learn that Peyton had been distressed, and that she had given Cody a letter and then sped off. It was a goodbye letter to him, and referred to, "when I'm gone."

We would discover she had written the letter that evening while watching a movie with Grayson, our fourteen-year-old son—and that, after she left the house, she had used her debit card to fill up her Mercury Mariner with gas. She also bought a pack of cigarettes—but she was not a smoker. We hoped she had just wanted to get away, temporarily, and would return soon. But, by the next evening, detectives were involved; a silver alert had been issued; and local news stations were broadcasting Peyton's disappearance and the surveillance video of her in the gas station. My wife, Mitzi, and I lay together on the family room sofa that night with hopes of seeing Peyton's headlights come up the driveway. We prayed, cried, and thought, "where would she have gone? … and why?" There wasn't much sleep.

The second day, July 19, was worse. No signs, no clues, heightened media coverage and our mounting anxiety. The detectives worked diligently and questioned many of Peyton's friends. Our days were long and our nights were longer. Our community, friends, and church—especially our pastor at Geist Christian Church, Randy Spleth—embraced us. Friends came over with food, helped clean our house, do our laundry, mow our yard—anything to lessen our stress. My good friend David ("Del") met me each morning on my front porch with coffee and prayers full of hope. Our friends didn't ask, they just did. People from all over the country sent messages of concern.

My heart was aching. Nobody had seen or heard from Peyton … and her cell phone's last ping had been close to our home around 3:45 a.m. or so on July 18—less than an hour after she had left Cody's and disappeared.

By day three, July 20, we organized a search party. Again the community responded. My dear friends Del and Chad mapped out routes, and volunteers met in front of Mama Bear's coffee shop that Saturday morning. On the evening of July 20, there was a prayer vigil at Holy Spirit Church. I tried to attend, but emotionally lost it driving to the church with Pastor Randy, as I saw the gathering of Peyton's friends—so I had Randy take me back home. We could hear their singing, from our house, and it gave us comfort knowing so many were praying for Peyton.

On Sunday, July 21, *Good Morning America* invited us to tape an interview that would be aired Monday morning. We prepared a written statement and had a family picture ready. Then, an hour before leaving to be interviewed, the detective stopped by and said he had a lead. He told us our neighbors in the cul-de-sac next to ours had found tire tracks, and a construction fence down, by their newly constructed home. The tire tracks went directly into Geist Reservoir—and matched the width of Peyton's Mariner.

I honestly can't remember much after that, other than Mitzi and me lying on the dining room floor together, grabbing hold to each other and any faith and hope we had left, as we waited for the police and dive crew to check the lake. There was a lot of commotion outside with police sirens and a helicopter from the news station. Our grief hit an all-time high when we saw the detective walk up our driveway with several officers. He confirmed Peyton's car had been found, with a body inside. They didn't have a positive identification that it was Peyton, but they didn't need to tell us any more. We knew our daughter would not be coming home. We would not be able to hug her again, or tell her we loved her.

161

Our new lives, our new normal, was beginning ... and a new grief that no one could have prepared me for set in. I'll never forget going out to get Landon, our nine-year-old son, who was playing football outside ... and walking with him around the back of the house, leaning down to look him in the eyes ... and telling him that Peyton had died. Tears rolled down our cheeks as we hugged each other. I hurt for myself, but I hurt for him more. I knew how close he and Peyton were. ... How could she have left Landon?? That was when new questions started racing through my head ....

Our family cried together and hugged each other tight for the next hours. One of the men who had walked up with the detective was the police pastor. We had two pastors at our side during our most needed time. Randy had come by our house about thirty minutes prior to the detective's news about finding Peyton's car. He had had a feeling he was needed (the Holy Spirit was working). I remember walking past our piano and noticing the song "Amazing Grace." I saw the words, "I once was lost and now I'm found," and read them aloud. I was glad that Peyton had been found.

We all slept together that evening in the family room. It was, again, a restless night of crying, praying, thinking and asking ourselves the many unanswered questions, especially, WHY? I'm not sure if it was this night, or before, but, in the middle of one of my sleepless nights, I got a sensation of complete peace, that Peyton was telling me she was okay ... she was happy again ... and I thought I even saw her face, smiling, in the window of the back door.... Could have been dreaming or even hallucinating, but it gave me a brief smile and some comfort.

Over the next days, Randy led us through the aspects of the memorial services and funeral. My parents and one of my brothers, David ... all from Kansas City ... helped me address elements I could not face on my own. David helped me make decisions regarding the urn, the niche, the services. I will always be grateful for David's brotherly love and strength during my most vulnerable time of my life.

And the obituary. I delegated this task to my dad and was so grateful he was able to do this for us, and for Peyton.

I struggled to grasp the reality of this situation and walked around in a state of exhaustion, confusion and disbelief. Stress and despair were taking a toll on my mom, as well. Suffering severe heart palpitations, she was admitted to ER with takotsubo cardiomyopathy—commonly known as broken-heart syndrome. She was in the hospital for two days. My poor dad had to ensure his bride of fifty-one years was stabilized, while he was grieving his granddaughter's death. A granddaughter he had helped bring into the world. He handled it with strength, courage and patience. He has always been my hero because of his actions of love.

The community—more than six hundred people—poured their love out during the visitation. With the help of Mitzi's brother, Landy, my good friend Mike, and the church personnel, we had several rows of pictures and memorabilia displayed. Four hours of hugging, crying, and praying with friends, family, even strangers from our community who had heard—and so, so, many kids who all loved Peyton. Mitzi, who was also devastated and struggling, did an incredible job of greeting the masses. We made it through the long evening with God's strong hand upon us and by the loving support of so many, including some we hadn't seen in years. We were so moved by those who had come. The number of high school kids made it even more emotional. They told us how much they loved Peyton, and that she was a great person with a gentle spirit and kind heart. My heart physically ached when I hugged these kids and tried to help them make sense of this horrific situation, when I myself was hurting and confused.

Prior to the public funeral service, we held a family service for the placement of the urn. I let Grayson carry the urn, and knew he would treasure that moment. At the service within Geist Christian Church, we came in to our dear friend Ryan Ahlwardt, director of Young Life, singing. Ryan did an outstanding job and was also immensely helpful in providing spiritual comfort to Peyton's friends and other youth. We were appreciative of Randy's eulogy as he gracefully addressed some of the tough topics around death, and especially suicide. He made us laugh with stories we had shared with him about Peyton; and he made us cry, as we said goodbye to Peyton.

Peyton's life began on March 6, 1995, in Overland Park, Kansas. She was delivered by her grandfather, my dad, Dr. Paul Riekhof. Peyton was a wonderful baby and brought so much joy to us. Her sister, Jessy, only a year older, was a second mother and Peyton's best friend throughout their younger years in Kansas City. We moved to Indianapolis in 1997, had our first son, Grayson, in 1998, and Landon was born in 2004. Peyton loved her little brothers and showed tremendous affection for them.

We had many fun trips with the kids: Disney World, Disney cruises, and renting an RV for two weeks to travel to West Texas. Peyton enjoyed these family vacations and loved adventure. She was also a natural, gifted, athlete. I have great memories of coaching her and watching her play the many sports she so loved. I will always remember one of our first times playing Wiffle ball, when she about took my head off with her first swing of the bat! She began playing softball at age seven. She played with passion, and loved the sport and her teammates. She wore #11 for most of her softball years, except in high school, where the numbers were pre-selected.

In high school, Peyton excelled academically, taking Advanced Placement courses and maintaining close to a 4.0 grade point average; but she started to withdraw from friends in an effort to avoid the girl-drama that is common. She was sensitive and wanted peace. Her love for softball also faded. Insecurities from insensitive coaching, and injuries—a broken thumb and wrist—contributed to her challenges. Her confidence plummeted during her junior-year season. She loved softball, but chose to stop playing.

Signs of severe depression took hold during her senior year. She struggled to sleep at night and to wake up in the morning. She started missing school. Eventually, I got the guidance counselor involved and we agreed Peyton would use an online program, and that she would go to Gallahue Mental Health Services to get help. Surprisingly, Peyton was receptive and, during this time, made a poster representing her future. It was so reassuring to see her smile when she presented it. She had cut out images symbolizing how she envisioned herself in the future: pictures of a husband, children, a home, being a dentist, etc. This was all very promising and gave me hope.

For her graduation, she had beautiful photos taken, and we had a wonderful party for her. I made a video, with many pictures and special music, and played it during the party. I cried during the video-showing, and afterwards Peyton gave me a hug, which I'll always treasure.

She was excited about her first year of college and through a website had found three roommates at University of Kansas (KU). In late June, we attended KU orientation together and I was excited to show Peyton my alma mater. However, she fought fatigue all throughout this trip, and I became worried again. After our return, we began shopping and getting Peyton ready for college. She worked as many hours as she could and also enjoyed helping coach Landon's baseball team. She spent a lot of time with Landon, taking him for ice cream at night, and on special trips, like to the zoo. During the second week of July, she sent me a text, excited about hitting $5,000 in her bank account, and I told her how proud I was of her. This was one of our last text exchanges.

Then came the week of July 15. A party involving some drinking started the week off in the wrong direction, but we believe facing the imminent reality of going away to college—leaving her friends and family—was the biggest trigger. And then, the evening of July 17 arrived. We will never know what she was thinking. We will never know "why."

The early hours of July 18 marked the start of my new life ... my new normal, with a broken heart that will never completely heal.

As our families and friends began to leave in the days following the visitation and funeral, our house became quiet and the sadness became real. I became lonely, and had too much time to myself to think. I knew the shock would wear off for others ... and that, as everyone went back to their lives, we would need to somehow start our "new" lives. But ... how do you go on with life after losing your daughter?

Mitzi and I knew recovery was going to be a long road, so we immediately looked into counseling. Randy continued his great pastoral care, and we had several references for Brooke's Place. We thought it might be good for our kids, but discovered it would be good for us, too, as they provide a support group for the parents of the children they're serving. The other group we found was associated with the American Foundation for Suicide Prevention (AFSP). We also got individual counseling started as fast as we could. Our counselor's compassionate style and gentle demeanor were perfect for us.

I poured my energy into trying to understand all I could about grief. Then about suicide and mental illness associated with suicide. I read books continuously—even throughout full days. To understand ... and to escape my sadness. Books about death, faith and heaven have also been helpful. I never knew how many books there were in which experiences of heaven are described. These books give me a reassurance, some peace, and hope of heaven and seeing Peyton again.

Along with therapy, I have relied heavily on friends I meet with during the week at Mama Bear's: Del, Chad, Fred, and Ben. My weeks are not the same when I miss these sessions. With these guys, I can be myself. We pray together and talk about everything. They help me more than they know, and I love them for just being there.

I found another group of friends when I received a package in the mail that included a letter and two books. The package was from Don Trainor, MD. He says the Holy Spirit led his actions to write the letter and send the books, but I know some of this was his own spirit, that is both giving and compassionate. One of the books was *Tuesday Mornings with the Dads*. Don invited me to a gathering with the "Dads." I thought about this for a couple of months, then notified him that I would attend. I showed up with the book in hand, asking, "Is this the group from this book?" I never imagined there would be twelve to fifteen dads there, who would tell their stories of loss until I eventually closed it out with my story about losing Peyton. I felt an instant connection with these guys, and their stories touched me deeply. They had lost their children in many differing ways: accidents, cancer, suicide, murder. All tragic, all unspeakably sad. I felt they each knew how I felt. I didn't need to explain anything. They shook their heads and understood where I was and what I was feeling. Just knowing I wasn't alone was comforting. I began attending as many Tuesday mornings as I could, and it's become an important morning for me and my healing. We share whatever is on our minds. We ask for advice on how other Dads have spent anniversaries or survived holidays. We genuinely care for each other and have empathy that nobody without our pasts could have. I'm incredibly grateful to Don, and hope to return the favor towards other dads who endure the pain of losing a child.

All in all, our counseling, support groups, and the many times I've told the story of losing Peyton, has helped me go through the grief, and heal. I've found I MUST go through it, and experience pain, to heal appropriately. I can't go under it, over it, or around it—and I especially can't ignore it, or it will cause great agony eventually, one way or another. Even regarding my physical health. I went to my primary care doctor a week after the services, as I had a constant aching of my heart (it felt like my heart was breaking!). He did tests and ordered an echocardiogram for the following week. He also put me on a blood pressure medication and an antidepressant. I did start feeling better, although my heart was broken forever.

Holidays are especially hard. At Christmas, we decided to get away. We went to Hawaii. On Christmas Eve, we set off lit-up flying lanterns—gifts from two of my colleagues (Cindy and Allison)—over the ocean, and shared happy memories of Peyton. Our church had also held a special memorial grief-service right before Christmas, during which Randy hugged and prayed with us, and we lit a candle for Peyton.

I also got a tattoo before our Christmas trip to Hawaii. I put "Peyton" above my heart with the letter t shaped like a cross. Peyton is always in my heart, with our Lord, and at peace in heaven. I know she was laughing at me while I got the tattoo, saying, "Oh my God, my dad is getting a tattoo!"

On March 6, 2014, we celebrated Peyton's nineteenth birthday by taking her favorite cake to her at the cemetery and having the kids release balloons with small notes written to her by each of us. We also gave a gift in her name to the Indianapolis Zoo. Landon, in particular, loved this idea.

Mitzi and I grieve differently, and that's okay. It was rough on both of us in the beginning, as we couldn't appreciate each other's ways and means. As time went by, we finally understood the differences. The key is counseling together. It forces us to discuss issues that might be hidden inside or that we're too proud or embarrassed to talk about.

Our children grieve differently, as well. Jessy struggled to get through the fall semester at IU, but toughed it out. Grayson has done well and talks openly about Peyton and how much he misses her. Early on, he questioned why God would let this happen. A natural and healthy question. Since then, he has accepted that God didn't choose this, and that Peyton took her actions under the influence of severe depression. Landon, with his young innocence, might be strongest of us all ... and brings us joy when we most need it.

As I continue to write this, it is now late summer and we have passed the first anniversary of Peyton's death. This summer both boys wore #11—Peyton's number—on their travel baseball teams. Landon hit his first out-of-the-park home run during his last game of the season, and I know

Peyton was smiling with pride and may have helped carry his ball over the fence at Billericay. What a great memory.... Our kids are so important and make it easier to deal with grief.

As we move forward, some things change, some remain the same. Peyton's room has her posters, her pictures, and her handwritten KU first-semester schedule still in place. This room is difficult for me to enter, but I did spend time there, crying on her bed, on her birthday.

Our very caring master-gardener neighbor helped us create a memorial garden for Peyton in our backyard. Like Peyton, it brings us much beauty, and is a place to find peace and solitude ... a place to pray and talk to Peyton. The butterfly has become our symbol for Peyton. This started the night after the memorial services—a butterfly flew around Landon and landed on his head and on my brother Tom's shoulder. A butterfly also landed on Mitzi's shoulder during the evening. They give us faith that Peyton released her pain (her cocoon) and is now a beautiful angel (butterfly) in heaven and with us always. The other day a butterfly flew around us as we sat in our back patio. It landed and let us touch it (her) ... not sure, but I think Peyton felt our touch and saw our sadness in missing her.

My faith has remained unwavering, and I have not felt anger at God. I do feel anger, but it's directed at the disease of depression, or at myself for not taking more aggressive action with Peyton. I know my personal guilt needs to be resolved, and I'm working through that. My faith has been my strength and where I go for peace and grace. Soon after learning of Peyton's death, Grayson asked if Peyton was going to hell because of suicide. This was something I had never wondered, but it was a good question that I put Randy on. I knew this might come up due to several religions that consider it a sin, and one that is unforgiven. Peyton had accepted Christ into her life when she went through confirmation. I had no doubt she was in heaven. Randy helped us understand that the Bible does not say anything about suicide as a sin, and that God doesn't judge on your final act. I know my God is one of grace and mercy, who took Peyton in with open arms of love and acceptance.

Peyton's legacy is to assist others who are struggling as she did. I've created a non-profit foundation called The Peyton Riekhof Foundation for Youth Hope, which provides funding for suicide-prevention training and organizes community-wide mental health awareness programs. We also hold an annual softball tournament called Play for Peyton.

Peyton will be in my mind and on my heart forever. I will always have four beautiful and wonderful kids: I have three here on earth, whom I love and cherish; and I have one special angel whom I love and still have a relationship with. As time goes on, the grief waves will crash with less intensity. I will treasure the memories and time I had with Peyton, yet keep my faith and family as my priorities, and continue to live in the present. My marriage will endure the differences in how we grieve, and we will stay strong through this, together.

My new life purpose is to fight mental illness, namely depression and suicide risks. For more about this, please see the "Resources" section in the back of this book.

I miss Peyton so very much, but I know she is making a positive difference in many people … including me.

Michael Riekhof

Thomas Peterson Stitt
December 5, 1977 – May 2, 2013

As I write this, I am struggling. With the passing of my son Tom, fifteen and a half months ago, and with writing about it. With writing about him … and about myself. I have spent four months making notes, taking frequent but increasingly daunting walks in the park, in search of…. Words. Hopeful, sad, sometimes angry. Confused. Overwhelmed. Planning, writing, crying. Thinking too damn hard. Tossing the notes, and starting over. Again. So I will try a new tactic. I will tell you outright, from a father to a listening reader, what I've been struggling with and failing to articulate in the more traditional narrative. But be forewarned. It is disjointed, fragmented, incomplete, and sometimes elusive even to me. I cannot promise you I will finish it.

First, I want to include a bit about MY difficulty … in writing this. Why that is, and the evolving feelings, including why I want to write at all. … However, those words are escaping me at the moment … and my mind wanders elsewhere.…

Reflecting on how our family was experiencing life on May 1, 2013 … the day before Tom passed … is where my thoughts go as I think about the past year. My wife, Cheryl, and I had been together for thirty-eight years. We both work as health care providers and enjoy our jobs. She is a speech pathologist and I am a pharmacist. We bought our house, and the ten acres of land it came with, when Tom was an eight-year-old.

Tommy had struggled in school with some issues but was obviously very bright. Answers were sought while theories and solutions were offered. Dyslexia, learning disabilities, ADD and other possible issues were raised. Tom as a child … before the teenage years and puberty began … seemed happy. He had friends and was close to a cousin who spent a lot of time with him. He was involved in 4-H at the county and state fair levels. He helped to raise and show sheep, although he finally came to me with the admission that he hated the experience and wanted to quit.

During these early years, we noticed some tendencies about Tom that seemed odd. He could become very fixated and even obsessive. On a fishing trip in Canada, he was drawn to fishing lures and their bright and varied colors. He would have loved to buy every one that he saw. This seemed harmless, although the obsessive nature of it made me wonder. He would turn this obsession to worry and eventual fear concerning weather. Every tornado season became more terrifying than the previous one, for Tom. The sudden, loud noises that firecrackers made were disturbing when the Fourth of July came around.

Our family grew as Tom entered his teen years. Cheryl became pregnant at the age of forty, and Tom's brother, Sam, was born. As we had watched Tom develop, and thrilled in his ability to crawl, communicate and take first steps ... we now thrilled in Sam's development....

Tom's teen years brought what we at first dismissed as simply acting out. He withdrew from us, seemed angry often, abused substances of various kinds and generally behaved as teens often will (and are famous for). There were happy times as well as the times that challenged us as parents. Tom had friends and certainly derived pleasure from many of these relationships. I feel that our family was always important to Tom. He could be a very kind and loving son, brother, nephew, grandson, cousin ... and enjoyed being in all of these roles for the first half of his life.

When Tom was twenty-four, and Sam was ten, our family grew again. We celebrated Thanksgiving Day that year by stepping off a plane in Indianapolis with our new two-year-old daughter, Lily. We were exhausted and glad to be home, but had loved being in China ... where we had adopted Lily. To say everything was new and different to her would be an understatement; but one thing she recognized immediately, from pictures we had sent, was her brother Tom. She called him "brother"—or the Chinese word for it—which thrilled him. Tom, with some help from a close friend of ours, had a Thanksgiving dinner ready for us that day. It was a remarkable day and the five of us felt balanced ... and like a complete family.

But there were still challenges, and as time went on and he got older, Tom's behavior became more erratic. It became more unusual. I have a clear recollection of discussing with Cheryl an incident ... and Tom's disturbing way of dealing with that incident....

... I want to talk about MY struggle to accept Tom as a seriously mentally ill person and finding myself thinking, "if only Tom would try a little harder" ... when intellectually I knew that he was trying his hardest. His great sense of humor and his intelligence sometimes blurred his mental illness in my eyes. I WANTED him to try harder, because I wanted him to be better ... to be happy ... and it was difficult (sometimes impossible) for me to accept the degree of his illness. ... What I remember so vividly, is Cheryl saying that she was beginning to really believe that we were dealing with mental illness, not terrible behavior. My realization of how serious and literal she was being shocked me. I didn't believe it at first. My struggle to totally accept this mental illness lasted many years. Cheryl and I accepted it as we could ... when we could ... as did other members of our family.

To the two of us ... to Sam and Lily ... the illness was just part of Tom. As time went on, his illness became Tom and Tom became his illness. The eventual diagnosis turned out to be schizoaffective disorder. Our son suffered the wide swings of mood that are present in bipolar disorder along with the complex profile of symptoms that characterize schizophrenia. His level of acceptance of the disorder was light years ahead of mine. With the benefit of hindsight, I see Tom's life as a daily struggle that he kept up for as long as his body would let him. The picture wasn't always pretty. The last year had some ugly and scary times. Cheryl and I struggled to set appropriate boundaries to preserve our family's health and sanity. Some radical changes in his "team care" concept were underway and we had reason to believe that ... at least in the short run ... the situation was going to improve.

These beliefs and hopes ended for us May 2, 2013. I was working when I received a call from someone at the care team's office. Tom had apparently missed a few appointments with various people. For him to do that without calling was unusual. They asked me when we had last talked with Tom. It had been about three days for me. As time went by, that afternoon, the calls kept coming and I attempted to reach Cheryl at her job. Tom's psychiatrist called saying she was concerned enough to order a "safety check." This would involve the local police going to his house to make sure Tom was in fact ... safe. As I agreed and verified that I understood, I hoped the unexpected visit by the police wouldn't frighten Tom. I tried to suppress the other fears that were getting stronger and louder in my mind. I tried to stay calm and keep my mind on my work. Eventually, I was on the phone with Cheryl; who called whom, I don't remember. She was telling me the police had sent an officer to the hospital where she works. I think my mind was trying to filter out what I didn't want to hear. I thought they were staying with her until word was given to us of his safety or that he was on his way to a hospital to be cared for. I finally clearly heard her say, "Larry, he's dead!" It had to be that stark for my mind to let it in. My pharmacy technician helped me lock up until another pharmacist could arrive. I left to meet Cheryl at Tom's house. The police and officials who were there could not have been kinder or more sensitive to our feelings. They told us that Tom was laying on his kitchen floor where he had fallen. They had cleaned him up a little ... from a cut on his head when he fell ... and covered him. We were told we could go in and see him if we wanted to. I wanted to remember Tom as I'd seen him last, but Cheryl wanted to see her son ... and touch him. She kindly told me "no" when I said I'd go with her. I appreciate that, to this day. An autopsy confirmed what the medical examiner's initial opinion had been that afternoon. Tom had died of a heart attack. His body simply couldn't go on any longer.

... I want to mention the genuine ... internal ... difficulty Tom had ... facing day to day life. The loneliness he must have felt ... the general fear of engaging in the outside world. His sense of always disappointing us (he was often apologetic), mixed with verbal rages that he unleashed on us and felt terrible about later. I wondered how he could ... and if he would ... keep fighting every day and not give up.

... I want to include that Tom had expressed his belief that no matter how verbally abusive he was with Cheryl and me ... that we would NEVER leave him or give up on him, because "we were a family." We were his parents. That statement made me angry when Tom was alive. I felt taken for granted. After he died, it comforted me to know that he was at least secure in HIS belief that we would always stand by him. Even if I hadn't been as sure.

... I want to share that I feel in a very real sense ... I had been grieving Tom's loss for years. Even before he was gone. ... Maybe the most surprising thing about losing Tom when he was only thirty-five ... was that I wasn't surprised. His mental illness had been profound and progressive. His "social anxiety" had gone way beyond that tame description. He had become a prisoner of that illness and the fear it had caused. Tom was a big guy, and his weight had just kept increasing. He got no exercise to speak of, took a staggering number of psych meds, was diabetic and hypertensive, and was a smoker. I hated his smoking, because I knew it was so bad for him. And yet his enjoyments had become so few—I hated that, too! I had wondered how long he would be able, or want, to go on living. I had worried about suicide when I thought about the never-ending nature of his struggle to ... "just live." When his heart gave out, I felt (and still feel), a huge range of feelings ... but not surprise. I feel guilt that I wasn't surprised, but guilt seems to be a feeling that is universal when parents lose children. The "what could have beens" ... the "if onlys" ... the "I should haves." They torment me.

... I want to mention that, for me, the visitation and memorial dinner had a powerful value ... one I'd never realized the family could experience. ... We chose to have an open visitation and, later, a smaller memorial dinner for our family and closest friends. Both evenings reminded me of happier days with Tom that had existed ... years that had been overshadowed by the more recent and darker times of Tom's illness. I discovered the value in having the support of family and friends while grieving. The reminder that we weren't alone in our loss was comforting beyond what I had expected. The pain was still there, but lessened when people allowed us to share it with them....

... I want to talk about how comforting it can be when people admit, "I don't know what to say." The feelings of helplessness that those words reflect is a helplessness I felt, and still feel, as well. Those words of helplessness sound like an expression of love.

... I want to talk about the individual journey that this grief has been for me. I've felt very supported by friends and family ... but I feel it is my journey still. A Dad in the first book, *Tuesday Mornings with the Dads*, got my attention when he discussed *doing* something ... *asking for help ... using tools and resources that are available.* These are action words and phrases and concepts that I've struggled with in other areas of my life. The help is there if I ask for it ... it's the asking that is so difficult for me. But that tools are there to be *used*.

... I want to share that, when my grief-related sleep deprivation affected my work performance, it resulted in taking time off to visit my sister—and that I learned that this was *okay*. That I was supported when I asked for help.

... I want to talk about the discovery of the Dads group through my friend Amy leaving me a copy of the first book. How I went to those first Tuesdays with an attitude that bordered on "fix me." And that I had felt frustration and even anger when I wasn't "fixed." ... I want to mention the dynamics of a group meeting and the benefits ... although it took time for me to feel those benefits. The Tuesday mornings have become a changing thing for me personally. My feelings have ranged from disappointment and even anger (because these men who had all lost children couldn't "fix me"), to a recommitment to the group by both the other men and myself ... which has allowed the Tuesday mornings to become a source of comfort and trust, and has transformed the ninety minutes, for me, into a time of peace and serenity. I feel this just by being there. When I speak and share, and even when I don't feel like speaking. It feels like asking for, and being, *helped*. I have learned something about the power of a caring group. Some days it is enough to simply get the hugs that come as we leave....

... I'd like to talk about how Bill Funke contributed to the group ... helped me ... and helped himself, on his own individual journey. How his death, and the feelings that were there, were shared by the group. Again, pain shared being lessened somewhat. ... Bill Funke had come into my life as a customer in the pharmacy that I work in. We made a personal connection that went beyond typical. "Let's have lunch sometime" turned into doing just that occasionally. Bill was a global businessman and his work took him all over the world. He had connections and friends in China—and had lit up when he found out that our youngest child, Lily, is Chinese and was adopted from Hunan Provence. So when Bill returned after two or three weeks travel and asked me how I was doing … I found myself being honest. Something seems to tell me the people I can open up to and not just answer "fine." I told him about my oldest son, Tom … and that we had lost him. Bill listened to me on that Sunday afternoon in front of the pharmacy counter and soon had tears running down his cheeks. He told me that he, too, had lost a son. Bill's son, Brian, had been about the same age as Tom when he died. The unresolved feelings that Bill had been left with came with him as he joined us on a Tuesday morning session with the Dads group. He said, afterwards, that he had come to support me, but had also found comfort that helped him cope with his own loss … still painful after twelve years. … We would lose Bill in less than a year from that first Tuesday. I still remember sharing the news of Bill's passing with the other Dads … and … again … feeling that my pain had been lessened because I had been able to share it. Bill's visitation and memorial service were attended by several of the Dads … many more sent prayers for his wife and family….

… I'd like to talk about some of the things I've learned, or am still learning: that we all grieve differently … certainly men and women … and that there is no correct way to grieve. That I can't "fix things" for someone else … no matter how hardwired I am, as a man, to want to do just that. That attempts to fix things make things worse and are doomed from the start. … That my world has changed. I can be happy again and laugh and enjoy life, but my world has

CHANGED. ... That guilt seems universal among parents left behind.

... I'd like to talk about having dinner with Mark and Deb Fritz after having attended the group for a short while ... that it was like a tonic and had a value beyond what I had expected. Mark had written about the loss of his son in *Tuesday Mornings with the Dads*. He and Deb made themselves available to Cheryl and me, and we had dinner with them several times. These were simple and quiet evenings that allowed Cheryl and me to talk, as a couple, about what we were experiencing. It was one of the first times we had done that or anything like it.

... I'd like to thank Mark for gently encouraging me to write and to participate in this project. He reinforced the idea that it might help me ... simply by sharing the fact that it had helped him.

There have been times when I have made this writing feel like the "high school assignment from hell." That feeling is of my own design and despite past experiences that have taught me the value in writing about my feelings. I was given encouragement by some of the other Dads on Tuesday mornings. Several close friends provided encouragement, too, simply by being interested ... and by listening. They listened as I described the frustrations as well as the relief I felt.

... I'd like to include some specific insight I received from other Dads when I shared that I was struggling with this process of writing.... There were two statements that came to me like gifts. One man said, "You know, you don't HAVE to do this if it isn't comfortable or helpful to you." That reminded me that I was doing this because I *wanted* to do it. I wanted to write this chapter, because I believed it might be therapeutic. ... The other comment that made an impact that same morning was, "In both basketball and in our lives, we miss one hundred percent of the shots we don't take." I began to think of writing my thoughts as an opportunity. ... And then there was Dianne's gentle coaxing that came as I was ready to give up writing.... She made me laugh out loud when she sent an email saying she thought I might be "thinking too hard." That statement was an absolute bullseye! She added a "how about this?" suggestion or two to help me take the pressure off of myself.

It is important for me to include this. The struggle. The support. The relief.

The gratitude.

... I'd like to thank this group of Dads ... men I am growing to trust and care a great deal about ... for the support I've experienced this past year, and for the care they've shown. And to my wife and family, too. I do not take them for granted. It does help me feel secure to know they are there. Perhaps this IS an individual journey, but I've never felt alone as I've moved forward.

The idea of grief being a journey is a concept that seems to work for me. Like most treks I've been on, this grief journey has had times when the road has seemed smooth ... with the wind at my back. But, it is a simple fact that coasting down a hill will eventually be followed by climbing up the next. The wind will sometimes be in my face. At times, constant feelings of loss ... fear and sadness about Tom's death ... have been intensified by other events. About three weeks after Tom's death, I lost a cousin. He and I had been close as kids, and had continued to stay in touch as adults, getting together for dinner when we could ... and going on a fishing trip in Northern Michigan every October. His death was unexpected, violent and horrendous. Losing someone in this way was an experience like I had never had.

The shocking nature of the crime resulting in my cousin's death also resulted in a change of my focus. What had been a laser focus on Tom and our loss, was now spread to include my cousin. Eventually feelings of guilt that I was not grieving for my son enough, or properly, set in.

I try to be gentle with people who are grieving. I've learned that when I encounter a grieving person ... I may feel powerless. I may feel that all I have to offer is a willingness to listen. My experience has taught me that, far from being powerless, that willingness to listen can be a powerful tool to give to a grieving person ... to a healing person.

I've learned that I need to be gentle with myself as well. My experience is all I have ... certainly not expertise. The grieving experience even within myself varies a great deal. Dealing with the loss of my dad, my mom, my brother-in-law, my father-in-law, my cousin ... and many friends ... has each been as unique an experience as that individual was. The process of grieving for my son is just that ... a process. The grief will always be there, as certainly as Tom will always be a part of my life. While "getting over it" will never happen ... things will get, and are getting, better. The healing doesn't happen in my time frame.

I do the best I can.

Among the many feelings I have about our son Tom is one of pure admiration. I admire the courage he showed every day as he kept trying. Even as his mental and physical health got dramatically worse ... he kept trying.

He did the best he could.

That's what Cheryl, Sam, Lily and I will do with this grieving process.

We'll do the best we can ... together.

... To my son Tom, I would like to say, thank you. For that lesson, and for the lesson in life about family ... and feeling secure. I also want to say, I love you. And always will. I'm glad you knew that.

There it is. That's what I wanted to talk about. Or at least it's a beginning.

Larry Stitt

Patrick Andrew Trainor
October 23, 1990 – March 21, 2010

Pat was a smart, fun-loving young man with his entire life ahead of him in 2010.

He had a lifelong love of animals, and during high school had volunteered at the Indianapolis Humane Society. This early experience led him as a freshman to Purdue University for animal science and pre-veterinary studies. He lived in the dorm, rushed for Beta Theta Pi fraternity and became a member. He had a B average after his first semester at Purdue and resolved to improve his grade point. He knew he would need to have a 3.6 GPA or better to get into veterinary school after his undergraduate education was completed.

Spring break of Pat's second semester at college, several of his fraternity brothers went to Florida for fun and frivolity. It seemed perhaps fortunate at the time, that he couldn't go, because he had a hernia that required outpatient surgery. The surgery was scheduled the Friday before spring break; this timing would allow him time to recover before the semester resumed.

The second Saturday of spring break (and over a week after his surgery), his fraternity big brother, who was leaving Purdue and joining the air force the next Tuesday, held a farewell party at his parents' home in Fishers, Indiana. With permission from his surgeon, as his recovery had been uneventful, Pat was allowed to attend. The parents hosting the party were home that night, but there was nevertheless significant underage drinking at the party ... apparently with their tacit approval. Around midnight there was a drinking competition and Pat ended up vomiting on himself. After cleaning up a bit, he was put to bed to sleep the night off. Sometime later, someone went to check on him and he was not in bed. His car was gone, too. The last ping sent from his cell phone to a cell tower had been at 1:22 a.m.

Pat was missing—with absolutely no clue where he was or what had happened to him. None of his friends at the party said they had a clue. It was a parent's worst nightmare. A massive manhunt ensued from Sunday through Wednesday, which seemed like an eternity at the time. It involved hundreds of people searching woods, ponds and roadways in and around Fishers, Indianapolis and West Lafayette (where Purdue is located). There was significant local news media coverage over those four days. A Facebook page dedicated to finding Pat was created; and news conferences were held, seeking the public's assistance in finding him. In the end, his body and car were found in a retention pond in the same neighborhood where the party had occurred. His blood alcohol level was 0.193—nearly two and a half times the legal limit.

We miss Pat dearly and so very much wish he were still with us. At the same time, we are so thankful he was found, so we could have closure regarding his disappearance, and so we can have a final resting place for his physical remains. We don't know why his life ended so abruptly, shy of his twentieth birthday. However, we do believe that God had a plan for him and for us. We also believe that his spirit, joyfulness, smile, love of animals, and fun-loving personality live on, in and through us.

The following is the eulogy I wrote for him, which I delivered at his funeral Mass on the day he was buried:

> Patrick came into this world the same way he went out—with *surprise*. His three older brothers were born twenty-two months apart, but then, after six years, Patrick was born. So his entrance into our lives was a *surprise*. Unfortunately, his life ended during his freshman year at Purdue University as a sudden surprise. In between, there were nineteen years of robust life, smiles, laughter and good times. There are many words and phrases that characterized Pat's life and time here on earth. These include:

Infectious, ever-present smile ~ People person
Fun-loving ~ Youngest child ~ Honor student
St. Monica Elementary ~ Cathedral HS
Carmel HS ~ International Baccalaureat
Purdue ~ St. Maria Goretti ~ Child of divorce
Wide circle of friends (male and female)
Son ~ Stepson ~ Brother ~ Stepbrother
Cousin ~ Nephew ~ Friend ~ Student
Catholic ~ Baptism ~ Confirmation ~ Cub Scout
Football ~ Basketball ~ Lacrosse
St. Vincent de Paul ~ Humane Society
Spanish-speaking ~ Green Mustang
Finish Line ~ Buckle ~ Eagles ~ Irish
Boilermaker ~ Tarkington Hall ~ Beta Theta Pi
Pre-Vet Studies ~ Pug lover ~ Brett Favre
Green Bay Packers ~ Aaron Rodgers ~ Colts
Clothes-horse ~ Texting master ~ Easygoing
Playful ~ Amazing ~ Confident ~ Loving
Sensitive ~ Affectionate ~ Caring ~ Cheerful
Enthusiastic ~ Joyful ~ Wonderful ~ Energetic
Optimistic ~ Excellent ~ Gentle ~ Adaptable
Reliable ~ Positive ~ Brave ~ Determined
Curious ~ Inquisitive ~ Gifted ~ Thoughtful
Outgoing ~ Beloved ~ Hardworking
Ambitious ~ Talented ~ Bright star
Missing ~ Facebook ~ Searching
News reports ~ Geist surprise ~ Tragic ending
Unfinished business

We never know when God will call us home.
We never know when that last
hug,
kiss,

hello,
good-bye
or text message
will be.

No matter how old you are,
life is sweet and short.
Love Family.
Love Friends.
Love God.
Love Life.

Holy Spirit ~ Palm Sunday ~ Easter Resurrection
Heaven

Don Trainor Jr., MD

Jason Nicholas Uhrin
March 23, 1990 – December 28, 2011

It is Tuesday, December 27, 2011, 9:27 p.m. I am driving home from visiting my mother, near Chicago, and my cell phone rings. It is a nurse at St. Vincent Hospital in Indianapolis. It is the call all parents fear.

"Is this Don Uhrin, the father of Jason?"

"Yes."

"Your son has been in an accident; I need you to come to the emergency room as soon as possible."

"What kind of accident?"

"A car accident."

"Is it serious?"

"Yes."

I explain I am on my way back from Chicago, that I am near Lafayette and will be there in about an hour. We hang up.

I drive. The questions race. The nurse had acknowledged that it was "serious"—what does that mean? Should I speed up? Should I be driving a hundred miles an hour? I decide that would be foolish and settle for 85 mph ... and return to the question. What does "serious" mean?? Surely not death—he's in the emergency room at St. Vincent Hospital, a top-flight trauma center—and medical science is amazing. ... Isn't "critical" more serious than "serious" ... and then it progresses to "stable," then "better," and finally "fully recovered" ... right? ... Could this be so serious that my son dies? I quickly replace that thought by circling back to "she said, 'serious.'" The questions don't stop, they expand. Visually. Horrific pictures join the scenarios filling my head: he's lost an arm; a leg; he's a paraplegic; oh my God—a quadriplegic; a serious brain injury—a living vegetable.... Oh my God.

I try to stop the images of tragedy from flooding my brain. I turn to prayer. I talk to God. In desperation, I plead. "Please dear God, be with and help my son through this—and Lord, please help me, too!"

When I arrive at the ER I am greeted by a nice man. He instantly recognizes me and asks, "Jason's father?" "Yes," I answer proudly. He tells me the doctors are still working on Jason and guides me to the waiting room, where Jason's mother and sister are already waiting.

I learn that both my son and his fiancée, Sydney, had been walking—they weren't in a car, they were *pedestrians* —crossing 82nd Street in Indianapolis, a couple of blocks west of Allisonville Road, when they were struck by an SUV.

They had been shopping and were on their way back to Sydney's apartment at Lake Shore Apartments.

My God, Jason AND Sydney both in the ER! Suddenly I notice, on the name tag of the gentleman who had greeted me … the word "CHAPLAIN." A chill runs through my body—Oh God, please don't let me lose my son—could this be that serious?

After a long wait, a neurologist meets with us. He explains that Jason has multiple injuries. The one he is most concerned with is the injury to Jason's brain from the impact. He explains his brain is swelling and the pressure building inside his brain is potentially beyond survival. *Did he say "potentially"?* He goes on to explain that he's drilled a hole in his skull to help relieve the pressure and has given Jason heavy doses of anti-inflammatory medication.

The doctor is talking in a way that clearly is not hopeful and is preparing us, coldly and pointedly, for the worst. "Your son may not survive this injury."

I stutter a question: "may not"?

There is room for hope.

"Doctor, can we pray together, now, that—with your help, the medicine, and God's intervention—my son makes it?"

We all hold hands and pray: the doctor, Jason's sister, his mother, the chaplain, and me—my son's father. We pray from the depths of our soul that Jason and Sydney be healed.

As the doctor is leaving I ask when he will know when things are improving. He says by 10 a.m. tomorrow. At that time, he will run a test to measure brain activity.

I'm finally allowed to see my son in the operating room. Several wounds and tears on his face have been stitched back together. Bruises cover his exposed body. I'm told by the ER staff that there are several broken bones—they will heal in time—but, it's the brain-swelling that is the critical issue. I note the change in vocabulary. This is no longer "serious." It's critical.

My boy, my son, my dear sweet Jason looks to be at peace. Tubes are connected everywhere—and he is on a ventilator—but he is *alive*. Thank God for that!

We learn that Sydney, Jason's fiancée, is also critically injured. She has been sedated and is awaiting surgery for a crushed pelvis.

I'm physically and emotionally exhausted. It has been a long day and night. A nurse encourages us to go home and rest for a few hours.

At home I sit on my bed. My body literally convulses. I cry from the depths of my soul—and pray to my God in heaven.

My thoughts go from Jason fully recovering—to dying—to being a vegetable for the rest of his life. Dear God, please help my son—and please help me—I pray in the name of your son, Jesus.

I am back at the hospital before 10 a.m.—I wasn't able to sleep at home. The neurologist and a team of doctors are going to test Jason for brain activity. All others are asked to leave his room while they do the testing.

Sydney is taken to surgery. Her condition is still critical—but her situation sounds hopeful.

Forty-five minutes later, the nurses call Jason's family back to his room. The neurologist addresses us with a firm voice and a stone cold face, and states, "I'm sorry, your son is gone—there is no activity in his brain. Your son is no longer with us—we pronounced him dead at 10:43 a.m., December 28, 2011."

How can he be gone? He is still on life support—his body breathing with the help of a machine—his body is warm—his skin alive—is he not still alive?

I ask the doctor, "is there even just a glimmer of hope yet?" His answer crushes my spirit. "Your son is gone—he is no longer with us—there is NO chance of recovery. I'm sorry, your son is dead."

Jason's mother, his sisters, relatives and friends, and I—we all sob and shudder and cry—our most precious Jason is gone. At twenty-one.

Physically and emotionally I am spent—I've cried myself out of tears. But my body still convulses, shakes, my stomach is turned inside out.

Everything has changed—I will never be the same again.

Following the pronouncement of Jason's death, we are approached, tactfully, by Michelle of IOPO—Indiana Organ Procurement Organization. She asks if we might consider having Jason give the gift of life to others through organ donation. I had never consciously heard of IOPO before, but my fiancée, Margot, had asked the nurses about the possibility of Jason being an organ donor ... and I knew there was a red donor's heart on Jason's driver's license. We had talked the day he got his license, about what being a donor might mean, and he had said, "Yes, of course ... I would want to be a donor." Knowing this, we, too, made the decision to donate Jason's vital organs. If there was no hope left for him to recover, we wanted to honor his desire, and hope that others might live as a result. We are advised that it will take twenty-four to forty-eight hours for the organ donation team to identify suitable recipients of Jason's organs, and to arrange for the multiple surgeries that will be involved.

Darlene of TheraPets also approaches us. She asks if we would like to have a therapy/bereavement dog sit with us and Jason. At first this seems a bit odd in a hospital room. But then Jason has a dog—his family has dogs. We like them and we know Jason does, too, so we say yes to TheraPets. The next two days we are blessed to have the presence of Max, a cute little Westie. Max seems to me to be like the Sphinx that guards the pyramids in Egypt—except Max is snuggled up and protecting and looking out with dignity after something far more precious: my son, Jason.

At 7:10 in the evening—a little over eight hours after Jason is pronounced dead—we receive news that Sydney has suddenly passed away. Her brain, too, had been injured, and swelled late in the day—and she, too, with Jason, the love of her life, is in heaven. God rest her soul, too! Jason and Sydney—peas and carrots—together this day with our Lord in heaven for eternity. Bittersweet. Sad beyond imagination that they are gone—yet happy they are together with our Lord and Savior. While I say this, I do wrestle with a degree of uncertainty, but pray earnestly that it is so, and that one day we will all be together again. In the meantime, it is a comfort to know Jason received the sacrament of the sick … last rites … before he was pronounced dead. It was important to me that he receive that last sacrament.

Eerily, Max the therapy dog is a supportive presence to all as we wait the next forty-eight hours for the organ-donation process to play out.

Suddenly, it's time. Friday, late in the evening, they come to take my boy and start the organ harvesting. Jason has lost his life—yet he is giving new life to as many as eight to ten people. I am proud of my son beyond explanation. To lay one's life down for the benefit of others is heroic. What higher gift can one give? Everyone who loved Jason is here to say goodbye. My sister writes a note to the doctors and we place it on my son's chest, along with a rosary, scapular, and St. Christopher medal. The note reads:

TAKE CARE DEAR DOCTORS OF OUR MOST BELOVED JASON. TREAT HIM AS YOUR OWN. MAY YOU BE GUIDED DURING SURGERY AND MAY THE RECIPIENTS BE BLESSED WITH LIFE. THANK YOU—GOD BLESS YOU ALL.

UHRIN FAMILY

The next time I see my son, he is in a casket at St. Elizabeth Ann Seton Catholic Church, for his funeral. January 2, 2012. My God, please accept my son into heaven—and dear God, help me and his family deal with our loss.

Nearly four hundred people visit Jason before his funeral Mass. The feelings of a father at his son's funeral are those of disbelief and hopelessness. I was supposed to die before Jason—not he before I. I remain crushed. Picture boards are filled with images showing my son at different ages—the story of his short life. Tables are covered with his memorabilia: hockey skates, drums, golf flags from the golf course he had worked at and loved; trophies from swimming; soccer; pinewood derby cars from Boy Scouts, and so on.

His Catholic funeral Mass is beautiful. It brings honor to his life and dignity to his death. At the end of Mass, I give the eulogy for my precious boy.

Since we lost Jason, I have reviewed his life … and the arc of it. He was gone so quickly: he steps from a curb—in a happy moment shared with his beloved fiancée—and is gone. With no explanation from the driver of the vehicle, and no understanding for us. An inexplicable collision leaves behind an unfinished life, with unanswered questions and unresolved challenges. They may have nothing to do with that night, but I am still contemplating them. I have always been someone who "makes things happen" versus "lets things happen" or worse yet, "wonders what happened." The reality of his death has me reeling over which of the three I was with my son.

The day Jason was born, I was thrilled. "I have a son!"—the perfect complement to my two daughters. How delighted and proud I was to have a son. All the things dads do with sons—I had been looking forward to it all.

As Jason grew up, his sweetness was clear and consistent. He was constantly hugging his mom and dad and always, always saying, "I love you, Dad." And always from his heart—not just a cliché of words.

Jason's young life had faced many challenges with school and an early diagnosis of ADHD. He was put on the medication equivalent of Ritalin. I can't help but wonder, did I do the right thing then? … He engaged in life fully. He seemed to thrive even, at least at times. He participated in all that he could. Hockey, soccer, swimming, marching band! He endured struggles and failures, but also success … and whether he was up or down, his unconditional love for his family, his warm hugs, smiles, humor—his sincere "I love you"—prevailed.

Eventually his grades started sliding, and he began having run-ins with the law.… And I began realizing that something was wrong, beyond the otherwise fairly common teen foibles. We transitioned from an arrest for marijuana and paraphernalia—Not my son, how can this be?—to intensive outpatient therapy (IOP) at Fairbanks Hospital. Not once, but twice, and then he became an inpatient—and then IOP again.

Hoping to get to the root of his issues and feelings … and get him back on the right path … I took Jason on several father-son trips, including to San Francisco … and Sedona, Arizona … and the Grand Canyon.

Our last vacation was a trip to Disney World in Florida. It was a "whole family" vacation with Jason's sisters and precious niece, Cat. What a great time—with lots of pictures and videos to remember that happy time. The words written by Paul Simon in the song "Bookends" rings in my ears: "I have a photograph—preserve your memories— they're all that's left you."

I still wonder about what happened the night of the accident. Was it a careless driver who hadn't seen the two of them? How could she not see two people crossing the street? Was she distracted by something … reaching to pick something up off the floor? Was she texting? Were Jason and Sydney careless in crossing the street? Had I failed to teach my son to look both ways before crossing??

The driver of the SUV that struck them had not been drinking, and no charges were filed. I have never spoken with her. Instead, I grapple with the guilt of a father not protecting his child.

While I do wonder, I'm brought back to the reality that knowing or not knowing does nothing to bring Jason and Sydney back. Regrettably, it is what it is.

I have heard it said that adversity doesn't build character—it reveals it. What profound "character" has been revealed from Jason's grandmother, his mother, his sisters, his aunts, uncles, cousins, and many friends. Thank you, all, for loving Jason and his family—and for being here for us.

Even with all the love—even in the midst of it—I still struggle. Jason's life is gone. No cards or flowers or gifts replace his presence. It is so nice of others to reach out with sympathy and love; but they can't possibly know how this feels—and I am thankful they don't really know how it changes everything. I feel so alone in my pain as a father who has lost his only son. Losing Jason has admittedly tested my faith in God. It calls him and his will for us into question. And yet, I think about God losing his son on the cross ... did he feel this kind of pain, too? Surely he understands what fathers go through—but then, Jesus is with his father forever in heaven. I struggle ... and hope that Jason and Sydney are with them, and that one day I will join them.

In the meantime, I thank God that the funeral director and a friend from Fairbanks Hospital made me aware of a group of dads who have each lost a child. They meet on Tuesday mornings. As they say, it is a group no one wants to belong to, and the signing-up dues are pretty steep: need to lose a child. OMG. ... I had paid those dues, and they had, too. So I went.

It was an odd feeling, getting ready to meet total strangers as I was carrying the greatest loss I've ever felt— and an odd feeling actually meeting them. As I came around the corner wall in the restaurant, I saw a group of eight or nine men sitting around a table. I stopped walking towards them as they stopped their discussion and looked up at me— as I was looking back at them. I'll never forget the feeling that washed over me. I felt connected to these men in a most powerful and palpable way. My God, I felt in an instant what their pain was; and I knew they knew mine as well. Total strangers who hadn't spoken a word to each other yet. I could feel—not sympathy, but true empathy.

When a new Dad attends, the group share their stories, each father taking his turn in telling of his son's or daughter's life and death. A couple of Dads have lost more than one child. Hearing the painful stories, and sharing the uncommon loss of children, is beyond description. When it's my turn to share my story of Jason if I want to ... there was no pressure to share ... I start, and try, but am overcome by powerful grief. My voice cracks, its volume breaks up. My body shudders and convulses again. Through the tears I tell of my loss, and share my feelings with these men who TRULY understand in a way that no others possibly can— only other dads who've lost a child. What an unnatural loss to experience.

It's so unnatural, there's no word for it. No new identity, to help explain to others, or to help redefine yourself. When someone loses a wife or husband, he or she is called a widower or widow. Lose a parent, and you're an orphan. But lose a child ... there's no name for that. There's a similar unnatural effect regarding time. When you lose a parent, you lose your past; when you lose a spouse or friend, you lose your present; but, when you lose a child ... you lose your future. My God, how I looked forward to, and planned for, Jason's graduation, marriage, his first home, his children and my grandchildren, our first beer together, fishing and hunting trips, combined family vacations ... and on and on.

But this is my new normal—and there is nothing normal after the loss of a child. Gradually I am becoming forever changed—or is it suddenly. Somehow, I lost Jason all at once—and yet feel like I continue to lose him in pieces over time, when I think of the things I can no longer look forward to doing with him.

The hole in my heart is so deep I cannot fathom it myself, let alone attempt to explain it to someone else. The loss is like losing a piece of myself ... an arm or a leg: somehow I find a way to go on with the loss, yet I am reminded everyday that something is missing. And had I had a choice, I would've lost a different piece of myself—gladly—to have my son live. It is only someone who has had the same experience who can understand it.

Writing about Jason, and about losing him, has been difficult. The emotion and grief reemerge. It scares me to share the darker complexities of his life, because I fear the stigma of an addict will overshadow the loving and sweet boy Jason was. Although addiction is a disease, society still paints a picture of individual and family failure. Although Jason and his family courageously and vehemently fought it—and many times overcame it to see growth—there was relapse. But we all tried, including Jason. As I write, I, too, cannot help but ask, how did Jason ever hook up with the wrong people? How did we as parents not see it sooner? And, I imagine the parents of those "wrong people" are asking the same questions. We, all, need to remember it is a disease, with the added danger of attraction ... *enticement* ... for the innocent.

Sometimes when I sit with the Dads on Tuesday morning, reminiscing about our children, I wonder if our kids who have passed are gathering around a table in heaven, reminiscing about their fathers. I wonder if they know how loving their fathers were to them—and that we still are!

When we experience losing a member of our family, the importance of those who remain is magnified. We talk on the phone more. We hug more. And when we hug, we hug with more earnestness. We use any and every opportunity to be together. Our family took a healing trip to the mountains of Colorado—and, oh how we missed our beloved Jason. When we see each other, we utter those most important words, "I Love You." We always have, but they carry more weight now. Each time I hear and feel those words, I remember saying them to Jason, too ... each and every time we got together, and then again when we left each other.

Elisabeth Kübler-Ross and David Kessler discuss in their book *On Grief and Grieving* the five stages of loss: denial, anger, bargaining, depression, acceptance. And there is a sixth step: giving back to those who may be at the beginning of their own grief process, and being there to support them as others have supported us. The value, comfort, and impact of the Tuesday morning Dads group is in effect this sixth step. We are here to receive healing, the best we can—and we are here to give back, to help others heal, the best they can.

I continue to experience unexpected grief attacks. It is like standing in the ocean, facing the shore, when suddenly a big wave comes out of nowhere and knocks me over—or, in the case of a grief attack, back to tears once again. I know many Dads experience something similar. With hope, these stories will help us come to terms with our loss—and help others one day, too.

It is devastating to revisit and reexamine Jason's passing, and I have struggled. But the kindness of our editor, and her dedication to stretching timelines, kept allowing for my story to be included. I am hoping it will help another father, in his journey of loss, to know there are others who do *truly* understand.

I also want to, in the sharing, memorialize Jason's life and existence, and *celebrate* it. I hope I can help other dads understand—and help myself accept it, too—that in the end, the questions and doubts and fears ... our insecurities as parents … don't matter. The child who was lost, was, is, and always will be *precious* … and that child will be forever loved and cherished by both the dad here on earth and the Father in heaven.

As I write this, it has just turned three years since Jason and Sydney passed away. I miss them and continue to grieve their loss. As the Aaron Barker song, recorded by George Strait, reminds us, "Daddies don't just love their children every now and then. … It's a love without end, Amen."

I love you Sydney and Jason. Always and forever…. 'Til we meet in heaven. Amen.

Don Uhrin

jascha trevor updike

March 3, 1985 – April 4, 2014

There is a little boy, I know his name
But I call him by another name.
I call him my peanut, because he is my peanut.
Do you know, this boy's name?

It's Jascha Trevor, his name is Jascha Trevor,
I call him my peanut, be-cause he's my pea-nut!
Jascha Trevor, his name is Jascha Trevor,
I call him my peanut, he's my peanut!
He's my peanut! He's my peanut!
My peanut! My peanut, peanut, peanut!

I used to sing that made-up song to my second child, Jascha (Josh'-uh), when he was little. I wrote little ditties for all five of my children when they were babies. This was his song. I sang it to him from the time he was born. When he was four or so, he used to argue with me when I sang it to him. "I'm not your peanut," he would argue, "I'm your chocolate chip cookie!" "Why are you my chocolate chip cookie?" I asked. "Because you LIKE chocolate chip cookies!" he proudly answered!

Jascha loved children. Once, when he was five, he sought out my wife, Melinda, who was working in the basement. He announced to her that he wanted to be a dad of 100 children! She told him that he might have trouble finding a wife who would want to have 100 children. He asked incredulously, "But *why?*"

As he grew, he continued to serve and work with children. In church during his teen years, he helped with the nursery. He befriended all of the children too old for the nursery, too. He played with them, created stories and games, danced with them, and had a great time.

In his twenties, after college, he worked for four years at St. Richard's School in Indianapolis as an after-school-care counselor and summer counselor. Sometimes I wondered if he loved playing with the kids, or if he just loved playing *like* a kid!

Jascha, at twenty-eight, came to our house in February of 2013, less than eight weeks before his passing. We were in our bedroom, so we called him upstairs when he came in the house. He ran up and, grinning, tossed a photo our way. It was an ultrasound photo of a baby. His girlfriend, Eleni, was pregnant and due in September, 2013. Jascha was giddy. He was excited to be a father and, over the next several weeks, spent a lot of time preparing to be a good dad. He talked about getting a better job, a safer car for the baby, and general planning ahead.

A few weeks later, on April 1, we had Jascha and Eleni up to our house for dinner. Baked ham was one of Jascha's favorites, and we made it especially for that night. We spent the evening talking about the future, the baby, the plans. As the night drew to a close, we walked them to the door. We both hugged Jascha and said I love you.

That was the last time we saw him.

We are a musical family. My wife, Melinda, is a fabulous singer and studied music, and I play several musical instruments, so it was no surprise that our five children all loved music and developed musical abilities. Jascha, the second of five children, wrote his first song, "The Cowboy Song," at the age of four! As an adult he played solo, traveled America, and later developed a band named jascha. He was well known in the Indianapolis area not only as a musician, but as a special person.

It's easy to know our children when they are growing up in our home. But once they move out, we don't know them in the intimate way we did while they were living with us. For example, Jascha collected mattresses around his sparsely furnished home. I thought his was a strange collection, but when I finally asked him about it, he explained he did this to provide a place for visiting musicians to sleep as they traveled through town. He also loved to cook breakfasts of pancakes and bacon for the bands! Matt Erler, a local writer and someone who knew Jascha well, wrote a special tribute, "Remembering jascha," for the blog *Musical Family Tree* (MFT). It captured Jascha's character beautyfully and was printed in *NUVO* a week after Jascha's passing.

≈≈≈≈≈

Boom! Boom! Boom! Boom! Boom!
Boom! Boom! Boom! Boom! Boom!

The loud banging on the front door—*pounding*, in sets of five—woke us up about 3 a.m. on Thursday, April 4, 2013. "Huh? What?" I got out of bed as the pounding continued.

I made my way downstairs and looked through the peephole in the front door. I saw an older man standing between two police officers. As I opened the door, I noticed the man was holding a Bible. I've seen this in movies and on TV. I knew what it meant. A million thoughts went through my mind as he began to speak, and I didn't really hear him because I was thinking, "Who are they here to tell me about? Which one of my five children?" The man spoke with a quiet, soft voice and identified himself as the chaplain of the Carmel police department. He asked if I was James Updike, father of Jascha Updike. He said, "Jascha was found unresponsive in his home and did not survive." My heart sank. I realized my wife was on the last few steps of the stairs, trying to hear.

I turned and moved closer to her and said, "It's Jascha." She didn't grasp my meaning until they came into the foyer and the chaplain repeated the message. Melinda fell back on the steps and cried, "No! No! No!" Shaking uncontrollably, she uttered sounds and moans and grunts that only a grieving mother can make. This went on for hours. We had been together since we were teens, and married thirty-four years, and I had never seen or heard her like this before. Her reaction, more than anything else, helped me absorb the gravity of what was happening; however, I was numb, in shock, and wouldn't feel the total impact until almost a year later.

As I led Melinda into the family room, the chaplain and officers followed us in. The chaplain kept repeating to us, "We serve a merciful God. We serve a merciful God." I was thinking, "Really?" and yet I knew he was right. We had served God for years, and our foundation was built on the Rock, Jesus. And yet it was conflicting to hear this news and trust God at this particular moment.

By this time it was about 3:30 a.m., and we began to ask the chaplain questions. He offered what few details they had at the time and then began to ask about our immediate family and where they were. We told him one son (Juddson) was at Purdue in Lafayette; one son (Jordan) lived in downtown Indianapolis; our only daughter (Jennasen) lived in Broad Ripple Village, in Indianapolis; and our other son (Jared) lived at home, but was house- and dog-sitting for some friends in Zionsville. Jascha's girlfriend lived in Broad Ripple. The chaplain advised us to let them sleep. It was going to be a long difficult day, and once we woke them and told them the news, they would stay awake a long time.

So Melinda and I began to make a plan for the day. We would call our oldest son, Jordan, first, and tell him; and then we would go to everyone else in person to give the news, and gather the family together, one by one, as we went.

The chaplain stayed until just before 5 a.m. After he left, I made the call to Jordan, and he wanted to be with us. He arrived about thirty minutes later and when he came in, we all hugged and cried. Then, about 6 a.m., we left on our journey to tell the rest of the family. We instinctively brought along our little three-year-old Jack Russell dog, Indie. We drove first to Jennasen's home in Broad Ripple.

When we arrived, I called her on the phone and let her know we were there, standing outside, and needed to see her. I'm sure she was surprised to see her parents and her older brother, too, when she opened the door. We went in, gathered around, and told her the news as the chaplain had said. This was even worse than telling someone by telephone. Her immediate reaction was scary, because we could see the shock on her face and the confusion of it all. She and Jascha had lived together, away from home, for five years, and had a special bond. We all hugged and cried together, and stood there for what was only a few minutes but seemed like hours. Jennasen quickly got ready and then asked if her boyfriend, Nick, could join us.

We repeated this scene as we picked up Eleni, Jascha's girlfriend and expectant mother of his child, also in Broad Ripple.

Now there were six of us in the van, heading up to Zionsville to pick up Jared, our youngest. It was a longer drive, and it was helpful that we had brought the dog, because it turned out that she was a wonderful therapy dog. Indie loved on everyone, especially when they were crying … a poignant lesson for us all.

We arrived in Zionsville around 8 a.m., and I was sure we would be waking Jared. By now we had a routine. The six of us circled around and told him the news as the chaplain had said. We all hugged and cried together until we were able to move on. We then left for our one-hour drive to Lafayette to pick up Juddson, our last family member to collect.

This would be the longest drive of the journey. It was a long, quiet ride.

We arrived in Lafayette and drove to Juddson's apartment. He was there but not awake, so one of his roommates let us in. I believe Juddson thought this was some sort of happy surprise, but that immediately changed when we spoke. Once again we circled up, hugged and cried, and helped him gather his things to come home. We left Lafayette knowing not only that we were facing more phone calls to extended family members, but that we also had work to do. We own a small balloon company and had five deliveries scheduled for the day that would need to be completed.

As we drove back to Carmel we tried to help Juddson cope. Of course we were all in shock, too; but even after only a few hours, it wasn't the same as the first horrific moment of hearing the news.

On the drive back, I reflected on my day so far. I had awoken to the sound of banging on my door, to be told that I had lost a son. I then had to console my wife, his mother, in her immediate and overwhelming grief. I had to call my oldest son on the phone and give him the news ... and then drive to all of my other children's homes and tell them the news in person, watch their shocking reactions, and try to be a strong, solid rock for them ... all the while breaking up inside myself.

I traveled around the city alone in the car during that day and over the months ahead, making deliveries. I found myself going through what I later learned was commonly called "scream therapy," pounding the steering wheel, crying uncontrollably, and shouting, "Why? Why? Why?" and telling myself, out loud, "I lost my son. I lost my son. I lost my son."

The feelings I felt during this time were unlike anything I have experienced before: emptiness, anger, pain, anger, suffering, anger. I'm sure there was more, but the shock overwhelmed everything else to a degree. Did I mention anger?

And while the emotional distress is to be expected, what I did not expect was the physical toll. At first I was able to get things done, but when the adrenaline wore off days later, I was just tired; physically drained. I didn't sleep at first and when I did, I woke up with fifty percent energy or less, and was ready for bed by late afternoon. This became a difficult cycle to adjust to.

Until the funeral we received a lot of attention from friends and family, but after that it began to wane. Family members began to fly back to out-of-town homes, and a large number of our friends didn't know how to interact with us, and so we were mostly left alone.

We had a niece in Nevada who, prior to all of this, had had a new baby, and Melinda and Jennasen had planned months earlier to visit. They were also going to see the Grand Canyon—something my wife had wanted to do all her life. The trip was to begin with a flight out of Indianapolis on Friday, which turned out to be three days after Jascha's funeral. The girls were torn. Cancel the trip or go ahead? As a family we decided they should go ahead. Looking back, that was the right decision.

On Friday afternoon, we were to pick up Jennasen from her work and head directly to the airport (she was allowed only three days off work). As we picked her up, she handed me a book. "Here, Dad, this is from a guy at work who lost a son; he thought you might like to read it." The book was *Tuesday Mornings with the Dads* and the guy was Mark Fritz, one of the earliest members of the original Dads group. I looked at the title and tossed the book into the back seat.

When I got home from the airport, I took the book up to my room and dropped it on my bedside table. I realized my wife and daughter were now going to be gone for six days. The only child still living at home was working double shifts at his restaurant job. My other children were back at home and school, trying to return to their own routines. I began to feel really alone, and the loss was starting to hit me harder.

I'm not much of a reader so I spent the evening numbly watching TV until I went to bed. The next day was Saturday and I didn't have work. I found myself trying to fill my time. I saw the book again and decided to give it a look. The book contained stories of fathers who had all lost children, and how they had found comfort meeting together. It took me a while to get into it, but I soon found that I could not put the book down. There was comfort in knowing that, even though I felt all alone as my world was crashing down, other dads had been there before me; and it seemed they had been able to move forward. Not move on, move forward. That was a real hope to me.

I finished the book in two days. I have since heard some Dads could not read it, or could read only one chapter a month. None of that matters. What matters is meeting other dads who understand. These guys "get it"! I found myself going to the very next Tuesday morning meeting, only twelve days after we lost Jascha. Mark Fritz had given me an email address, and I let him know I would be there. He in turn contacted other Dads to ask them to come support a new Dad in his loss. It was both a horrifying and tremendous experience! I soon learned the common routine of a new Dad is to sit in the parking lot for five to ten minutes, trying to work up the courage to go in, and then finally go in. This is exactly what I did!

At the meeting each Dad had the opportunity to tell the story of his loss, and I had the opportunity to do the same, which I did. This was not a requirement; a Dad could pass if he wanted to. I found this encounter to be unexpectedly cathartic. It was refreshing—and seeing these Dads who were two, five, ten years or more down the road in their loss, gave me hope that I could live my life again someday.

I learned there was also a Thursday meeting south of Indianapolis, in Greenwood, and I went there as well. I felt I needed to attend both groups to maximize my exposure to these men who had so much to offer. After visiting both for a few weeks, I decided to attend the south side. It was much larger, and I needed to hear from a large group of men. More Dads provided more input. I didn't talk much during the first four months or so; I knew I was still in shock and I knew I just wanted to listen and watch their interactions with each other. I held out hope that someday I would be able to simply carry on a normal conversation. I hadn't expected to also be able to laugh again.

Over this time, I began to pick up valuable insights from the group that I could take back to my wife and my entire family. For months after the loss of Jascha the family gathered together every Sunday, and it was during these times that I would share what I was learning from the other Dads. These insights and tidbits from the Dads group included lessons learned; resources, such as books to read and the support of other families suffering through loss; and how to remember your loved one in many ways. The Dads also gave us a heads-up—that the second year would be harder than the first. "How could that be?" I wondered. But then I learned that the numbness of the initial shock can last six, eight, even twelve months! For me it was about ten months. During this period, I could work, perform my job, and do other things out of habit. But once the numbness phase passed, and reality set in, it became more difficult to function.

As my personal world became more challenging, so did my social world. Melinda and I had discovered that most people who haven't experienced the loss of a child don't understand the impact it has. They don't know how it changes a parent; how nothing will ever be the same; how it affects everyday life both physically and emotionally. Knowing these Dads and being able to talk about these challenges—and hear what works for them—has been invaluable to me, and to Melinda, and to our family.

The Dads group has been a tremendous part of my life without Jascha, and I cannot imagine going through this trauma without this group. I feel fortunate that I could attend so soon after my loss. I know some dads first come to the group years after their loss, and that it is hard to do, but that it is still beneficial for them. For me, well, I guess I needed the group from the start.

God knew that.

When Melinda and I were married, we had our favorite Bible scripture engraved on each other's rings. Her favorite verse was, "And we know that God causes all things to work together for good to those who love God, to those who are called according to His purpose" (Romans 8:28). Mine was, "Trust in the Lord with all your heart, and lean not on your own understanding; In all your ways acknowledge Him, and He shall direct your paths" (Proverbs 3:5,6).

After Jascha's passing, I began to try to see how these verses applied in our current situation. I am not going to go down that road here, but I want to give a few concrete examples of God's mercy that simply amaze me and reassure me of His love.

In late January of 2013, my youngest son, Jared, was driving home from work on a Sunday evening and was struck head-on by a drunk driver. The car was totaled. Jared was hurt only slightly, and not hospitalized overnight; but he was driving our car, so our car was totaled! Over the next couple of months we shopped around and, in March, 2013, bought a van that was only a year old. Our old car would not have been able to accommodate our whole family, but this van was able to on April 4—the day we learned about Jascha and drove around to pick everyone up.

Also, my daughter "happened" to work at a small office where Mark Fritz worked. He knew exactly what I was going through. He knew what Jennasen was going through, too, because he also has a daughter. He shared the book *Tuesday Mornings with the Dads* with her to give to me— and, through this book, I connected with the Dads who have become such an important part of my life and who continue to help us on this journey.

There are other scenarios, too, that have been too meaningful to be regarded as mere coincidences. I played golf in high school and college, but gave it up when we started our family. Many years later, when the older boys were out of college, Jascha and Jordan took up golf and we began to play together. These are some of my best memories with my older boys. We had been playing together for a few years, but when Jascha passed, I thought my golfing days were over. I couldn't even think about playing golf again. Then right before Father's Day in June of 2013, only six weeks after Jascha passed, Jordan invited me to play golf on Father's Day. I hemmed and hawed that I didn't think I could. I called a few local courses to try to get a tee time for Sunday morning, Father's Day (the busiest day in golf). We ended up at a local course only a few miles from home and, since there were only two of us, we were paired with another two players to make a foursome. As we were on the driving range warming up, we could see the first tee. It was about our tee time, so we went over and only one of the two other guys was there. He was a young man, probably close to my older sons' ages. I introduced us and asked about them. "Oh, my friend couldn't get out of bed this morning! I guess it'll just be the three of us."

"OK. Well, what's your name?" I asked him.

"Oh me? My name's Josh."

And then I immediately remembered the chaplain's words, "We serve a merciful God."

Jascha's baby boy was born in September, 2013, five months after Jascha's passing. It was a bittersweet moment in our lives. Exciting but sad … knowing how much Jascha loved children, and knowing he would never meet his own son. But we learned Jascha would nevertheless carry on the tradition of a father composing a song for his baby. Almost a year after Jascha's passing, on March 15, 2014, a memorial concert, "Last Honest Man," was held at Radio Radio to honor Jascha's life and music … the proceeds were to benefit his son, then six months old. Shortly before the concert, I found, in one of Jascha's notebooks, a lullaby he had written.

In his easy way, he had embraced the role of daddy … and, in effect, shared it with all fathers … including me.

As I had sung my song to Jascha, my peanut, I now sing his song to his little boy, his buckaroo. And I also think of Jascha as I sing it:

THE DADS GROUP

go to sleep, my little buckaroo
when you wake up, we'll do
what grown up cowboys do
we'll ride the range together, in fair or stormy weather
go to sleep, my little buckaroo

Jim Updike

FOUR STORIES

BY

FATHERS WHO WERE FEATURED IN

Tuesday Mornings with the Dads

Marc William Douglas-Larrison
May 11, 1982 – September 26, 2005

My name is Rick Larrison. My son, Marc, passed away on September 26, 2005, at the age of twenty-three. I found out about the Dads group on September 29 and attended my first "Tuesday morning" on October 4—a mere eight days after Marc had passed away. I knew immediately these meetings would become a necessity in my life. When I came to the group, I was drowning in a sea of despair. These men didn't just throw me a life preserver, they jumped into the horrid waters with me and guided me to shore.

When this book is published, I will be in my tenth year since I lost my son. In these nine years, I have missed only nine meetings. In the beginning, I was going to the meetings for myself. Now I am going because of a desire to pay it forward. I never want a Dad who is having a tough day to show up and have no one there to talk to. It has become my mission, a calling I feel obliged to answer. My weekly meeting with the Dads also keeps my memories of Marc fresh.

Because I have been a "constant" since joining, I have seen the ebb and flow of attendance, and the impact of both spreading the word—and showing up. When our first book, *Tuesday Mornings with the Dads,* was published, there was a core group of ten to sixteen Dads who were there regularly. In the time since, five have moved out of the area, and one now spends part of each year in Arizona. Several have job-demands that prevent them from attending the meetings as often as they originally did. But the book introduced our existence to a new group of dads who decided to join us— and many have arrived carrying the book.

At one point, the Tuesday attendance dwindled to one or two newer Dads and me. The impact isn't as effective with that small of a group. So one of the Dads wrote an email challenging the group (himself included) to make attendance higher on their priority list, and the group responded. Since then, the Dads present have varied from meeting to meeting, but there have been, fairly consistently, six to eight each week. This is a perfect size for the group to have one ongoing conversation that everyone participates in. When the number increases above that level, multiple conversations start occurring simultaneously. This is okay, too, but it fragments the otherwise collective experience.

Shortly after we published the first book, two of the Dads—one who lived on the south side, and one who lived in downtown Indianapolis—decided to meet with another dad they knew, who lived on the south side. They began meeting on Thursday mornings at a Bob Evans in Greenwood. That group caught on like a wild fire—and within a month or so they had a regular attendance of eight to ten Dads. This group now meets at a Denny's in Greenwood. They are still going strong and have a core group who attend every Thursday. On Thanksgiving morning they have a special tradition: they each bring pictures of their children and pass them around and talk about their sons and daughters. I attended their gathering one Thanksgiving, and it was a delightful time of sharing and hearing wonderful memories of each Dad's child.

One of the Dads who moved, Chuck Findley, initially moved to Scottsdale, Arizona—which is where another, Jerry Toomer, spends part of his year. Mukks Mukkavilli, a dad who had read our first book and contacted us, also lives in that area. Those three started meeting occasionally—and were joined by Paul Jankowski, the uncle of my pharmacist, Amy. When Paul lost his daughter, Amy sent him a copy of our book and told him she knew me. Paul sent an email thanking her, and said how much more he had gotten out of reading our book than from any of the other grief books. He also sent me a very nice email detailing how much comfort he had received from the book. It is posted in the blog section of our website http://tuesdayswiththedads.org/. Paul's niece Amy (my pharmacist) has become a big distributor of our book. She has handed out several books to family members and friends who have suffered the loss of a child.

There are many stories of how the first book has been linked from one person to another, and has spread from one geographical location to another, across the United States. The common remark we hear from men grieving the loss of a child, is that they got more from our book than any other ... mostly because the stories were expressly **not** written from a psychiatrist's or theologian's perspective. The stories were written by men who had actually experienced the loss of a child. No matter how our children died, we all have the same hole in our hearts, and any dad who has lost a child understands. That hole will never heal.

Along with the forming of the group, its expansion, and the exponential reach of the book, there are more specific, more personal, effects—unexpected blessings—that have resulted.

When I wrote my chapter for the first book, I indicated that many people, including my mother, could not understand why I was not getting over the loss of Marc. After my mother read the book, it opened her eyes to the fact that the loss of a child is far harder than the loss of a parent or spouse (both of which she has experienced). She no longer says things like, "You have to get over this and move on with your life." My brother has told me several times that he was in fear of losing his brother. He was seeing the same behavior in me that we had witnessed in our mom when our dad passed away—except I was not moving forward. He has always been one of the people who, though he has not lost a child, has nevertheless "gotten it." He attributes much of my current, more stable, self to the influence of the Dads group. Am I the same person I was before Marc's passing? In a word, "NO." But I am surviving, and evolving. As we Dads move forward, we each recreate ourselves and form a new persona. Our "new normal." But to have that is a blessing. It is a new way of *existing*.

Through the years since Marc passed away, I have had to create new rhythms and adjust old habits to cope with my loss, and these changes have helped me move to my "new normal" persona. Marc was my golfing buddy from the time he was about six years old. The first few times I played golf after his passing, I'd have tears in my eyes most of the way home. I thought, "I love playing golf. I have to figure out how to play without feeling the crushing grief afterwards." I decided I would play golf with Marc. I'd talk to him as I played. I figured, since he is now an angel, I'd ask him to help me with difficult shots. I'd say, "Okay, Marc, help me get through the edge of this tree," or, "help me get over the sand trap...." Well, I tried it and it worked. I can now play golf without the grief afterwards. Our symbol for Marc is a dragonfly. Whenever we see a dragonfly, we know Marc is there watching over us. I almost always see a dragonfly while playing golf. When I do, I always say, "Hi, Marc."

As I mentioned in *Tuesday Mornings with the Dads*, Marc was a blond and he loved blond jokes. He once said, "I'm a blond, so I'm allowed to tell blond jokes!" He knew a bunch of them and knew exactly how to tell them to get the most laughter. I now also love blond jokes. They bring back fond memories of my funny man. All of the guys in the group know this, and I get blond jokes in my email inbox quite often. Even my mom sends them to me. Hers always say, "Here's one Marc would have loved."

Marc had one of those portable basketball posts, backboard and rim. He set it up just off our driveway. You could tell he went out and shot hoops often, because of the wear pattern on the backboard paint. That post is still in the spot where Marc set it up. The net is now missing and most of the paint has disappeared from the backboard. Perhaps someday, when I need a project, I'll repaint the backboard, get a new net, and shoot some hoops occasionally. Whether I do that or not, that post will remain where it is.

I've found there are several other practices I've added to my routine, purely in remembrance of Marc. They are "for" Marc, and they help me cope, too. For example, we live on fifteen acres, and there are a couple of places on the property where Marc liked to spend time. One is a secluded flat area toward the middle of the property. He pitched a tent there, that he apparently used as a place to call his friends or just go to think. In Marc's memory, I mow this area several times a year. It is also where I buried Marc's cat when she passed away from old age.

Also on our land, is a regulated county drain. The drain pipes are buried until they get to the back corner of our property where they create our creek. Marc used our golf cart to go back there to study, think or just relax. I mow the path back to that spot because I know Marc would like having the path passable. I have thought, several times, that I'd like to build a bridge over the small valley that is just before a concrete wall where the buried pipes open into the creek. I think I would extend the bridge-decking over to the concrete wall to make a large deck overlooking the creek. It would be a beautiful place to go sit and read, write, think or just relax in the shade. It would be the greatest place to go and talk with Marc....

... I will never "get over" this loss. But, I am finding ways to balance my moments of grief with moments of peace.

Richard K. Larrison

Jake and Travis Findley

Jake October 31, 1994 – February 3, 2007
Travis July 1, 1997 – February 4, 2007

BEYOND THE NUMBING FOG OF GRIEF:
UPDATE ON THE JAKE AND TRAVIS FINDLEY STORY

It's the summer of 2015. Hard to believe it has been eight and a half years since I lost my only sons, Jake and Travis, in an SUV/train accident that occurred at a railroad crossing in Greenwood, Indiana, in February of 2007. At the time of the accident, I had no idea how I was going to survive a single day, let alone several years. I felt like I was in a numbing fog, trying desperately to escape it and come in to clear blue skies.

What I have found is I never really escape it. There is always a deep sadness and emptiness that I am constantly reminded of … not only through my own feelings and emotions, but through people and places I encounter daily. I search for some kind of normal life, and fight to get back to the person I was. But that never happens. I've learned that no matter what, I will never be the same. It's just not possible. My life has been divided into two parts … *before* the accident and *after* the accident.

Becky may have captured that phenomenon perfectly in an interview we did with Channel 13 in Indianapolis, when she said, *"The person I was doesn't exist anymore. I have to become a new person … I have to become someone else."* It didn't hit me until later how profound that statement was. There are times, when looking at all the great pictures we have, Becky and I notice that our smiles and eyes *before* the accident look different. We look happier and living life like it is supposed to be lived. Don't get me wrong, we can still find happiness and purpose in life, but it is simply different. Life *feels* different. There is a huge hole in our hearts that never goes away, and we've had to learn how to carry that with us every single day. We can't "move on," but we are figuring out how to manage the grief as we pick up the pieces and start living again … and somehow find a way to keep going one day at a time.

Speaking of pictures, one of the stark realities of all the pictures we took, is that there is a point in time where they just stop. That's how we will always remember the boys. No new pictures to take. It all stopped with a tragic halt. But, we are so thankful for all the pictures we do have, as well as all the treasured videos. Seeing those beautiful smiles and shining eyes looking back at us makes us smile back. The videos bring them back to life, and it is amazing to hear their voices, see their smiles, hear their laughs and watch those moments that take us back to some of our greatest memories. But it's just as easy to have tears rolling down our cheeks with these reminders of what we are missing so much. Even after several years. In reality, we know it will always be this way ... ALWAYS!

I think about all that I have missed already. Eight and a half years have gone by. Travis would have turned eighteen in July and Jake would be twenty-one in October. The milestones of life—like becoming a teenager, getting a driver's license and graduating high school have all passed by now. Jake would be a senior in college and Travis would now be a senior in high school. It's hard to comprehend, and I'm always imagining what they would have looked like as they got older. My mind can definitely do a lot of creative thinking, and sometimes I try so hard to figure out what they would look like and what they would be doing now. But when I come back to reality, I have to let those thoughts go, because it really does no good to wonder.

There is not a day that goes by that I don't think of Jake and Travis several times a day. I miss those boys with the same intense love I had for them the day they left us. To be able to hug them, laugh with them, play ball with them, tell them I love them.... Just to touch them. I would give anything just to be able to hang out and talk, to be their dad again, watch them grow up and become young men, to be the one they leaned on when experiencing life.

I've never been a big gravesite person. Of course, there are days I feel the need to go there and sit and talk to the boys or just pray. Any time I am in town, I make sure I spend some time at the gravesite. One time I took a lawn chair and their iPods along and listened to a bunch of the songs they liked. I sat there for what seemed like several hours. That gave me a lot of peace. But the main reason I don't like to go is ...

every time I look at that headstone and see their names on it, I just shake my head. It doesn't seem real to see their names there, to know they are gone ... and that, no matter what, it will never be the same ever again. It's a knife in my heart. It cuts deep and it always bleeds.

Here's what I have learned over the last several years. Grief is evil. It knows no boundaries. It takes you and spins you out of control into an unknown world in which you have no idea how to navigate. You are in complete darkness, trying to right yourself and fight your way into the light any way you can. Even if you find that small ray of light, there isn't a manual or template on how to contend with grief. You feel completely helpless, as if you have lost a battle with the world and there is nothing you can do about it.

I believe it was the unknown world of grief that caused Becky and me to have trouble. We grieved differently and seemed to have no idea how to help each other. Instead of being there to help guide each other through our worst and darkest days, we began to isolate and grow apart. That distance, and in large part the fog of grief, led to our unfortunate divorce. We didn't think normally, we didn't act normally, and we had no idea how to live life anymore. I believe if we could have persevered through the initial fog, we could have helped each other more than we ever knew.

Having divorce pile on top of grief is not a good recipe. They are two different types of grief that can be highly combustible if not handled with extreme care. And even when managed, they are an oppressive pair. I needed to be free of the constant reminders that seemed to suffocate me and prevent me from finding happiness. In my first attempt to gain some breathing room—and literal space—I moved to Zionsville, Indiana, which is about forty-five minutes or so north of Greenwood. It was far enough away that people didn't know me. I didn't run into people who knew Becky and me as a couple, and as parents. And I didn't have to drive by the physical locations that always reminded me of the boys and the great and horrific memories. Some may say I was running from the situation, and that may be a fair statement; but I looked at it as taking action—to save myself from going totally insane. Something had to be done.

Being in Zionsville gave me some relief, but I eventually decided to move clear across the country, to Scottsdale, Arizona; and then, because of an opportunity to work with my brother John, I moved further west to San Ramon, California, where I live now. Moving across the country was a chance to have a fresh start, maybe the chance to finally find happiness again, and to embrace the possibility of new beginnings. Whether in a new job or relationship or … whatever. It was the opportunity to find something concrete and tangible that may last for what I have left of my life.

But it was also a move that eventually revealed a lot of feelings I wasn't expecting. It was after I moved across the country, that the fog finally started to lift. I could look back at the early days following the accident and see that I hadn't handled the challenges in positive or effective ways, at least not when it came to my marriage. It was after moving here that I felt true regret at letting my marriage fail. I regretted that I hadn't done everything possible to have Becky and me stay close to each other through those first years of grief … even if silently and respectfully … so that we might have emerged from the other side of the tragedy still together. Those first years are by far the most difficult.

The good news is, Becky and I have been able to forgive each other and now can talk in open and honest conversation. We've been able to discuss things we could never talk about, before, while going through our most intense moments of grief. In fact, we've realized how important it is to talk, as we are the only ones who know the bond each of us had with our boys, and the only ones who can truly reminisce about some of our best days with Jake and Travis. She has even reminded me of special memories—little quirks or funny things the boys said—that I had completely forgotten about. Our talks have been a real blessing and very healing.

If there is any advice I would give to a couple who have lost a child, it is this: 1) You and your spouse will grieve differently. That's a given. 2) Be there for each other—but also give each other the space needed to grieve how you each need to grieve. 3) Respect the other person's grief—unless they are doing unhealthy or harmful things to themselves, physically. 4) Talk about your grief with your spouse. They may be desperately and silently wishing you'd stay with them … even if you aren't saying a word at times. 5) Remember, your spouse might say and feel crazy things. No matter how crazy, do not discount it in any way, because they are grieving, too. You might not understand it right then, but you will later, when you both can communicate more rationally. 6) Be patient, and never give up.

I don't have any idea what God has planned for me now, but I put my complete faith and trust in him to guide me every step of the way. God let me do some things my own way and let me discover some valuable lessons the hard way. He has now answered many of my fiercest prayers as I have been seeking answers for a few years. I'm thankful he has allowed me to see beyond the fog of grief.

There really is no way to explain the devastating and life-changing pain of losing a child, or children, to anyone, unless they have been through it. Although they can imagine what it might be like, no one else can possibly understand, unless they have experienced it themselves. This is why the Dads groups are invaluable in their support, advice, understanding, and in a brotherhood that lasts a lifetime. We have learned that the most educated grief experts, counselors and psychiatrists haven't been able to help us like we can help each other. I believe, in most cases, it is because they haven't suffered the pain personally. The Dads groups have literally saved lives. All hope was lost for some men until they found our group. Being a part of this unique brotherhood was one of the best decisions of my life after losing my precious boys.

Some more helpful words of advice, for friends and family of those who are grieving: don't expect someone who has lost a child to "get over it" or "move on." Losing a child is an endless journey. Also, don't expect them to eventually be the exact same person you always knew. It is impossible. There is a saying that "time heals all wounds." That is a false statement. Time and healing don't apply in the death of a child. Yes, healing will occur, but to be completely healed … just won't happen.

Here is something I know and believe in my heart. There will be many events in life that we will never understand. Maybe we aren't supposed to understand why so many bad things occur in this world. What I believe, however, is that all of this is temporary, and one day … one day … there will be a glorious reunion that will wipe away all of our pain, sorrow and tears. There's a song by the group Kutless called "I'm Still Yours" that sums up how I try to live, regardless of what has happened or what will happen. A portion of it goes like this:

If I lost it all, would my hands stay lifted
To the God who gives and takes away?
If you take it all, this life You've given
Still my heart sings to You

When my life is not what I expected
The plans I made have failed
When there's nothing left to steal me away
Will You be enough for me?
Will my broken heart still sing?

To my boys, Jake and Travis—

You two gave our family so much joy and happiness. Your smiles, laughs, caring nature, crazy and goofy ways and loving spirit live on in all of us every single day. My commitment to you both is to let your positive spirits live on in me for the rest of my life, until the day I see you again. I will forever love you both!

Chuck Findley
Romans 8:18

Ralph Nicholas "Nick" Fritz
January 5, 1980 – June 28, 2003

As I write this, next week will be the twelfth year since Nick's death. I had to think about the date and the years. This means our Dads group is now eleven years old. Wow! Time flies.

I see a thirty-four- or thirty-five-year-old adult and wonder what Nick would have looked like. What would he be doing now? Would he have cleaned up? I just wonder ……….. and miss him.

Nick has evolved in my memory from a young kid who died due to his drug addiction, to a man with an easygoing swag, a kind heart, an athletic free spirit ... who is no longer here with us. This evolution in thinking about him has been a slow process. I was so mad and burnt-out due to his drug use, that it took me a long time to think kindly of him. I had to focus away from how he died to how he lived. And he lived good. I am proud of the good I saw in him.

He is still alive on the other side and still active with me and all of his family and friends. That has been an important message from Nick—that there is life on the other side. He has revealed himself many times, many ways. He has firmed my own understanding of life and death. He has given us many gifts but this has been a big one.

I have heard other Dads talk about losing one child to death and other children to the process. This has been true in our family, also. A younger sister has followed Nick's drug use with her own and lost her relationships within the family over the twelve years that have passed. Other siblings have withdrawn and have been slow to reengage with various family. The dynamics of a family get-together have been difficult to maneuver. We have moved to individual outings and events with our children. I suspect I may never get all of my family together again for anything.

The Dads group has been a lifesaver. I have been active all eleven years—first with the Tuesday group, then also with the Thursday group. A group of men meeting with no leadership, no rules, no standards, no subject for discussion. Can't happen. I have asked friends, why does this group go on? Why do people still show up? How long will this continue?

Since our first meeting the only thing we have done for sure is tell our own story. When new Dads attend a meeting, we all tell our story. This lets everyone know they are in the right place, that they belong. There is never any question about belonging after you hear the stories. Men who have lost children. There are no good stories. And after hearing other stories, I am always pleased that my story is so mild. I always leave a meeting thinking I have it good compared to so many others.

What happens after telling our story, is different every meeting. Method of death, funeral service, cremation, burial, songs, speeches, comments, siblings, spouses, time, sex, friends, money, and on and on are discussed. No order, no time limits. Just free discussion. And we also discuss sports, politics, and whatever is happening in our worlds. We discuss events, fundraisers, law enforcement, the judicial system, holidays, special dates and family events. We check in on the quiet members and remember birthdays and death dates. We remember. We relive. We rehash. We cuss. We pat each other on the back and we hug. Great big bear hugs right out in public.

And the groups go on. Expand to the south side, to Scottsdale, to men we don't know in cities we don't know. Some ask to be on our email list and never attend. Others have quit attending and get upset when they find they are off a list.

A group of men who get it. A group we don't want to belong to and yet can't quite stop attending.

Churches send men to us but we are not religious. We pray and cry and laugh and love. Brothers. Brothers we did not know and now know too well. Brothers we understand. Hurt we know. Pain we want to forget but must speak of first.

Pain shared is halved. Too simple?? Maybe not.

I have now moved to working individually with Dads who may or may not be part of our groups. I have found

Dads who have served as confidants, sounding boards, and shoulders to cry on.

My friends have evolved in their own thinking about Nick. Hesitant for many years to discuss him or my groups, they now ask freely about the groups and talk about Nick as we discuss their kids and current events.

What does all of this mean? Nick never dies; he is in our thoughts and actions daily. My own pain is lessened. Not gone, but less. Changed I am. The change was immediate. I will never be Mark Fritz again. I think the change has been for the good; some don't, but I like myself better now and I love how I think and act towards my kids and grandkids. Life has gone on. I live with the loss of Nick inside my head and body, always there, always to be managed.

I cry often now. Every time I hear of a child dying. I think of the family and extended family. The dynamics that spin out of control in all directions. I cry for the lost child, the lost family, the dad and mom, left holding a bag of shit that will not stop stinking.

And I hope. I hope for the day this madness will stop. The day no child will leave this earth ahead of their parent.

And in the meantime, I hope that parents who face such a loss can find other parents who understand. Dads and Moms who will be lifesavers for each other, as the Dads have been for me.

Mark Fritz

Michael Edward Toomer
May 13, 1980 – July 21, 1999

Dreams are gifts.

Dreams remain for me the most vivid way of connecting with Michael after fifteen years. It was July of 1999—it seems like yesterday, and it seems like an eternity.

In my dreams we may be traveling, listening to music or working a crossword puzzle together … or battling with an insensitive high school teacher about Michael's need for some extra time to complete exams. Whatever the dream is, it connects me with Mike.

My dreams about Michael occur less frequently now than they did in the first few years following his passing, but they seem to occur more regularly when I am traveling, sleeping in a new place, a different bed. I'm not sure why travel triggers more vivid dreams. Do I simply sleep more lightly and dream more intensely, in general? Or, is it because we traveled together as a family very regularly...? Am I experiencing being with Mike on yet another trip?

While awake I largely have control of my conscious thoughts; but in my dreams I have no, or little, control. My painful feelings of losing a child come naturally and deeply. I am pulled more deeply into grief, penetrating layers and feelings I did not know existed. And, even though I have no control, and though there is pain, there is also healing and peace. There is the satisfaction of addressing the longing of wanting to be in touch, to be close, and to experience him more fully once again.

This is my new dimension of life with Mike.

We don't "work through grief" like people "get over" an illness. We don't come out healed; we become different. We can crash through the lower layers of grief and remain there. It is a choice. But, in our best selves, we strive to find the strength to live into that which our children would have wanted us to be. We double down on life and vulnerability rather than withdrawing and insulating ourselves from pain. Having experienced the worst that life can throw at us, we meet the challenge by surviving it ... and recommit ourselves to living.

I spend part of my year in Indianapolis and part of my year in Arizona. To the Dads in both places, I can deeply say, "thanks." They understand the loss of a child even though our scenarios may be dramatically different. For more than ten years we have shared a place to have coffee, a space in which we can laugh or cry. It is a table around which we can debate the merits of the Colts or Pacers this season, or where we can celebrate anniversaries of our child's passing, or the day of their birth, or share a memory from our past, or a wish for our future. To my son, "gone" fifteen years, I say this …

Michael,

I miss your smile, your dry sense of humor… our walks with Muffy, listening to Red House Painters … watching a particular Star Trek *episode (yet again) or looking up an obscure word in the dictionary in the living room.*

For the first couple of years after you passed, I thought of you "all" the time: I could hold two thoughts or feelings in my head and heart simultaneously; I did not want to let you go.

I now accept that you are gone … but you are still present each day, each moment, in some small way. The black onyx ring that you purchased in Malaysia fits well on my finger and reminds me that I hold a part of you close, and dear.

And yes, my dreams of you can be so real, and such a vivid way to feel connected with you. They are gifts.

May the Force be with you.

For those of you who have lost a son or daughter … do you dream? Do you talk with them silently, or even out loud? Do you write to them, or about them? Do you set off fireworks in their honor or fly a kite on the beach as you did when they were small, or place flowers at their grave?

When you find a way of connecting, do it.

Find your ongoing connections with your child; embrace them. *Go with it.*

They are gifts.

Jerry Toomer

CLOSING THOUGHTS

&

RESOURCES

What to Say—and Not Say— to a Grieving Parent

Parents who have lost a child experience the worst grief that can be imagined. For those who have never lost a child, it is unfathomable. Nevertheless, friends often hope to say something that will be meaningful, or at least supportive— and it is usually very simple to help a person who is grieving: give some time, listen, and say, "I am sorry." It isn't necessary to say more than that. In fact, saying much more, while well-intended, will possibly create more pain than peace.

There is a rapidly growing number of articles appearing on the Internet, addressing this issue. Most are written by a grieving parent, and some are quite pointed. While we, as grieving dads, nod our heads in agreement ... we are also grateful for the compassion shown by others, and do not want to discourage anyone from reaching out. We are offering this chapter—our variation of "what not to say"— because, although we believe others mean well, many truly do not understand how trite, insensitive, and even hurtful, some of the more common sentiments feel to a grieving parent.

We'll give a few examples ... starting with statements that credit God for the loss of a child: "God needed your child more than you did.... God has a plan.... God needed another flower for his garden.... Your child is singing and dancing with Jesus!" Although these are all well-meaning comments, they can ring hollow and diminish the tragic and life-altering event that a parent has experienced. Even, "Your child is in a better place." This basic faith-based sentiment might seem harmless, but it can be especially difficult for a grieving parent. Many of us are deeply connected to our faith, and it is our faith that does help us through; but, within those first horrifying days, we do not feel our child is in a better place. We are the parents—our child's place is with us. Similarly, we do not believe God needs our child more than we do. We do not believe our child's death was some kind of grand plan that God had designed for him or her. "The Lord works in mysterious ways" insinuates that God was responsible for the child's death—and for the way it happened. A more secular version is "everything happens for a reason."

We understand that people are trying to be comforting, and that as soon as they mention heaven or God's plan, they feel that makes it better. But it really doesn't. We are too numb to think anything "good" about the death of our child. No matter how strongly someone tries to justify it through a supernatural plan, nothing—in a moment of devastation—makes any kind of sense. Not even God. "Have faith and God will see you through this" can be helpful … but it can also feel like another way in which the child's passing has been trivialized.

Another category, mentioned by Angela Miller in Still Standing Magazine (January 20, 2014), includes virtually any statement that begins with the phrase, "at least." We, too, have heard our own variations. "At least you had them for the time you did.... At least you have other kids.... At least you had a child—some people never have children.... At least they will not suffer here in this world anymore."

Taking it a step further is the suggestion we should be thankful: "Be thankful he (or she) was a good child.... Be thankful your child did not suffer long" (we hear this statement even when the child experienced a particularly brutal scenario).... "Be thankful you have other children." Again, there's the insinuation that if we do happen to be blessed with more than one child, that makes the loss less painful or more tolerable. And, "You can always have another child." ... This implies our child is replaceable.

Along with urging the grieving parent to see the bright side, there is a tendency to prod the grieving parent to move on, cover up, or ignore the pain. As time passes, we sometimes feel pressure from friends and colleagues ... and even from other relatives, and the clergy. We might hear:

"You need to get over this."

"Don't let this destroy your life."

"Your child would not want you to suffer this way."

"Let go and let God."

"You need to stop thinking about your child; put away photos and other things that remind you.... Don't go anyplace that reminds you...."

Please try to understand ... we do not want to avoid our child. These memories are what we have. Even though some of them may be painful, we want to remember. "Time heals all wounds." But with the loss of a child, and with wanting to remember all that we can, so many activities and experiences in life re-open the wound and return a grieving parent to the pain. Miller states, "Not all wounds heal, no matter how much time passes. Not every wound turns into a scar. Not all suffering ends in this lifetime."

Other times, friends might try to soften the pain by trying to identify with our struggle, but the reality is they cannot help but approach it from ignorance—from not knowing. "I know how you feel ... my mom died a couple of years ago." They don't know. We have lost a child, not a parent. And we didn't know the distinct severity of this grief, either, until it happened to us, to our families. There is no "equating" the grief of losing a child. The loss can be fathomed only when it has actually been experienced.

We understand that these remarks ... all of them ... are sincere offerings to those who are grieving—but many of the consoling sentiments we grew up hearing, and repeating, are not the healing balm we've imagined.

Again, we are offering this chapter as insight for those who wish to support a grieving parent. We do not mean to discourage anyone from reaching out. Many of us still run into friends, family members and colleagues who do not know what to say. Those first words can be the hardest. But one of the most common mistakes is to refrain from saying anything at all. Do not be afraid or hesitant to approach a grieving parent to offer your condolences and support. While it is easy to unwittingly make an unfortunate comment, we do appreciate those who make an effort and those who help us enjoy the memory of our child. Sure, there may be tears and intense emotions, but that's natural. Being able to talk about the child, or children—some parents have lost more than one—is critically important ... not only in the early days of grief, but forever ... whenever we feel the need to share a certain memory or story. We loved, and will always love, that child with a depth and tenderness that only a grieving parent can know.

Of course, parents may not want to talk about their child at a particular moment and that should be respected as well. Certainly, if it is too uncomfortable for a grieving parent to have a full conversation, try to be aware. One can let the conversation be diverted if that seems to be desired, and the parent will usually take the lead in doing this.

It should be acknowledged, not all grieving parents have the exact same needs, but we recommend keeping it simple until you know what the needs are.

Miller suggests a good way for a person to help another who has lost a child is to say, "I am with you always." She ends her piece with this: "My child died. I don't need advice. All I need is for you to gently close your mouth, open wide your heart and walk with me until I can see in color again." Yes. Be with us. Keep us in your heart. Do not underestimate the value of just being there for someone who is in grief. It will make all the difference in the world. That's really all we need. Even if it is just to sit with us in these darkest hours and not say a word. Otherwise, what seems to help most is to say, "I am so sorry."

We are thankful that most people do simply say they are sorry for our loss … and we are thankful to know that most friends want to be here for us. We appreciate that you are taking the time to read our stories, and to get to know our children … and that you care enough to learn more about what to say—and not say. These are the genuine gestures that will help bring genuine comfort.

Thank you.

The Dads

Losing a Child to Suicide

Losing a child is the worst experience imaginable.... Losing a child to suicide carries an additional dimension of grief, an additional layer of wrestling with the self-torment shared among grieving fathers ... "I'm the father, I should have protected my child, I should have fixed this, I should have done that ... I should have prevented it."

I am sharing, here, additional detail regarding my own experience, for others who are grappling with such a loss—and also for those who are grappling with the fear of it. I hope the insight will reassure parents who tried so hard to help ... and shine a light for those who are seeking help.

Many people have asked me when we noticed any changes with Peyton and when we became concerned about her. We didn't see Peyton's depression until high school. Specifically, her junior year was tough on her. Different people experience different symptoms of depression. Peyton showed many of the warning signs but constantly fought going to counseling. We struggled with this reaction, so we looked for counselors who would be a good fit for her and her personality.

Peyton was very sensitive and didn't like turmoil or drama. She was quiet and did not want to discuss anything with us—and believe me, I tried hard to dig into everything, which only annoyed her. She had been an A student but began struggling to make it to school. We had to call the school MANY times to excuse her absences. We finally ended up taking her out of school and enrolled her in an online program, with the agreement that she'd also go to Gallahue Mental Health Services for help. At Gallahue she began to open up about her depression and seemed to be dealing with it in a positive way—and was thinking about the future. It felt like she was making tangible progress.

My wife, Mitzi, and I also went with Peyton for a family counseling session. This session included the three of us plus two counselors. Peyton shared how she felt when we said or did particular things. We tried to help her understand what we meant and that we didn't understand all that she was feeling during her depression episodes. She cried, we cried, and we all said we loved each other. I told her that, no matter what, we always loved her unconditionally. This was a good session for all of us. I look back and wish we would have continued with more of these group sessions.

As the school year ended, Peyton decided to stop going to the behavior program and we agreed she was doing better. She worked almost five days a week as a hostess at Stone Creek restaurant—a job she thoroughly loved. Soon, we celebrated her high school graduation, and she was excited about college. As of early July, two weeks before she took her life, we weren't seeing any signs of severe depression, only the same habits: staying up late at night, sleeping late into the day, moodiness, and generally what many people would think of as normal for a teenage girl. Our biggest concern was that, like many kids in their late teens,

Peyton was drinking alcohol. For the most part it seemed in control. But she knew of our disapproval, and so she sneaked it in when she could. I realize now that her drinking was a coping mechanism, but the alcohol likely contributed to higher levels of depression.

We will never know if something triggered her suicide. I do believe that Peyton was scared; that she didn't understand why she felt so hopeless and overwhelmed with sadness. I do believe that she didn't want to die but wanted to get rid of the pain. I believe she wasn't thinking clearly or rationally. She had assured Mitzi, only three months prior, that she would never kill herself—and even explained why, and discussed the future she was looking forward to: she wanted to be a mom, she wanted kids, and she could never leave Landon, our youngest.

When we lost Peyton, I delved into readings on grief. After that, I went after trying to understand suicide and mental illness associated with suicide.

We understood very early that Peyton died by suicide and we have never denied this to ourselves or to other people who have asked. The word "suicide" was tough to say at first, but I can say it now—because it's real and, unfortunately, it's all too common ... and because it's not talked about enough in a way that it should be. I often hear people talking about suicide in terms of someone having acted selfishly. In fact, it is a persistent view held by many people in our community. Personally, I believe Peyton had an incredible amount of courage to do what she did, and that it is shamefully inappropriate to call a child's death "selfish." It is both unconscionable and dangerous when we start judging people who, for whatever reason, are at the depths of despair. This is one of the main reasons for the stigma that surrounds suicide, and why parents and families who are devastated by it are reluctant—and effectively not allowed—to grieve openly.

We must avoid the association between suicide and "crime" or "sin." That's why I don't say "commit." I don't blame people when they say "commit suicide," but I do correct them and say that my daughter didn't commit a crime, she died by suicide. It was depression that drove her to a dark place and caused her to give up hope. It was a terminal illness. I just wish somebody would have told me, warned me, or even scared me, about the serious consequences of depression.

One of the ways in which I continue to heal is through my new life mission of helping others who are living with depression or mental illness. As I mention in my chapter, I've created The Peyton Riekhof Foundation for Youth Hope, which provides funding for suicide-prevention training and organizes mental-health awareness programs. Please visit www.thepeytonriekhoffoundation.com for more information.

While my focus has been on helping teens, depression is a danger for adults, as well, particularly regarding parents who've lost a child. Depression in this context is situational, precipitated by a devastating event; but treatment is still crucial and can be approached according to the individual's needs—via counseling, support groups, or pharmacological treatment, such as antidepressants. Regardless of the scenario, depression needs to be taken seriously.

Following, are key points and resources I share in a presentation offered throughout the community. My primary source is the American Foundation for Suicide Prevention.

Michael Riekhof

SUICIDE ~ DEPRESSION ~ MENTAL HEALTH
RESOURCES*

Most suicidal people don't want to die.
They want their pain to end.

*Approximately 80% who kill themselves
have given definite signals or talked about suicide.*

Warning Signs

*sadness • anxiety • desperation • emptiness • hopelessness
guilt • worthlessness • helplessness • irritability • restlessness
unrelenting low mood • pessimism • psychic pain
inner tension • withdrawal • sleep problems*

Other Common Symptoms

*fatigue • loss of interest in activities previously enjoyed
problems concentrating, remembering information, or
making decisions • disruptive behavior
loss of appetite, or eating too much
thoughts of suicide, or suicide attempts
aches, pains, headaches, cramps, or
digestive problems that do not go away*

Observable Signs of Serious Depression

*increased alcohol and/or other drug use
recent impulsiveness and taking unnecessary risks
threatening suicide or expressing a strong wish to die
making a plan • giving away prized possessions
purchasing a firearm
obtaining other means of killing oneself
unexpected rage or anger*

You Can Help.

Intervention: Three Basic Steps

1. Show you care.

Take ALL talk of suicide seriously. If you are concerned that someone may take their life, trust your judgment! Listen carefully. Reflect what you hear. Use language that is appropriate for the age of the person involved. Do not worry about doing or saying exactly the "right" thing. Your genuine interest is what is most important. Be genuine. Let the person know you really care. Talk about your feelings and ask about theirs.

2. Ask about suicide.

Talking with people about suicide won't put the idea in their heads. Chances are, if you've observed any of the warning signs, they're already thinking about it. Be direct in a caring, non-confrontational way. Ask about treatment: Do you have a therapist/doctor? Are you taking your medications?

3. Get help.

Do NOT leave the person alone. Reassure the person that help is available—and that you will help them get help. Encourage the suicidal person to identify other people in their life who can also help:

family members • favorite teacher • school counselor school nurse • religious leader • family doctor

Outline a safety plan. Make arrangements for the helper(s) to come to you—or take the person directly to the source of help. Once help is initiated, be sure the suicidal person is following through with appointments and medications.

If **YOU** are in CRISIS
Text: CSIS to 839863
Call: 317-251-7575

24 hours a day • 7 days a week • confidential • free

Mental Health America
http://www.mentalhealthamerica.net/

DEPRESSION is Common.
Reach Out. Get Help.
You are not alone.

• *American Association of Suicidology*
http://www.suicidology.org/

• *American Foundation for Suicide Prevention*
http://www.afsp.org/
Annual event: Out of the Darkness Walk

• *National Alliance on Mental Illness*
http://www.nami.org/

• *Society for the Prevention of Teen Suicide*
http://www.sptsusa.org/

• *The Jason Foundation*
http://jasonfoundation.com/

• *The Jed Foundation*
http://www.jedfoundation.org/

• *The Trevor Project*
http://www.thetrevorproject.org/

• *To Write Love On Her Arms*
http://twloha.com/

*Primary source: American Foundation for Suicide Prevention.

Mornings with the Dads, Inc.

Mornings with the Dads, Inc., is a not-for-profit 501(c)(3) charitable organization which serves dads who are grieving the loss of their child(ren). There are no membership dues, membership "rules," or expectations regarding attendance. Proceeds from book-sales support the group's mission and outreach, and financial contributions are tax-deductible.

Contact us at
E-mail: morningswithdads@gmail.com

For additional information and resources
Website: www.tuesdayswiththedads.org

Like us on Facebook! "Mornings with the Dads, Inc."

Meeting for Coffee — 52 Weeks a Year

Thursday Group—on the South Side
Time: 7 a.m., Thursdays
Location: Denny's in Greenwood; I-65 & Main St.
Address: 1253 S. Park Blvd., Greenwood, Indiana 46143
Thanksgiving: We bring photos of our children to share.

Tuesday Group—on the North Side
Time: 7 a.m., Tuesdays
Location: Le Peep restaurant in Castleton
Address: 8255 Craig St., Indianapolis, Indiana 46250

Please visit www.tuesdayswiththedads.org *to confirm times & locations of these and other Dads Group gatherings.*

"Mornings with the dads"

Thursday "South Side" Group

Front, L-R: *Jim Oxley, John Longworth, Dave Cook, Don Buxton, Steve Allen;* back, L-R: *Henry Pawlik, Jim Nathan, Rick Rhoads, Marv Habicht, Zach Ortman, Mark Fritz*

Tuesday "North Side" Group

Front, L-R: Larry Stitt, Jack Hill, Rick Larrison, Ed Kassig, Don Uhrin, Jim Updike; back, L-R: Don Trainor, Jerry Toomer, Mike Riekhof

Dads who have contributed a chapter but are not pictured: Greg Brown and Kurt Kriese. Chuck Findley appears in his chapter-photo, on p. 229.

L-R: *Mary Ruhana, Mary Oxley, Joan Sheppard, Janet Julius, Mary Lou Habicht, Debbie Heidelberger*

The Southside Moms Group

My name is Mary Lou Habicht and I lost my son Nicolas on May 23, 2004, when he was twenty years old.

Shortly after my husband started attending the Dads group, I decided to start a Moms group for grieving moms who have lost a child. Reaching out to others is a way of dealing with my own loss. I find it therapeutic to spend time with other moms who understand, and I hope those who attend the gatherings find it comforting, too.

We meet for dinner once a month at a local restaurant in the Greenwood area, just south of Indianapolis. We are a group of moms who all have the same broken heart, but sharing our stories helps ease the pain. We are here to support each other as we move forward step by step. Although we are all at various stages in our grief, we understand what each mom is going through while dealing with a loss like no other. The ladies in the group have all become good friends.

If you are interested in attending one of our dinners, please email me at marylou1711@gmail.com.

Legacy Funds & Fundraising Events

These are some of the recent projects that have been created in honor of the children of the Dads group. Please visit tuesdayswiththedads.org for more information and listings.

Adam Brown

The Adam Brown Award via Columbus Youth Hockey

Columbus Youth Hockey, with the Columbus Icemen, present the Adam Brown Award, recognizing the mental attitude-/sportsmanship of a graduating senior who is a member of the Columbus Icemen high school hockey team.

Adam Brown Memorial Golf Outing

First Friday in May, in Columbus, Indiana. Proceeds benefit Columbus Youth Hockey; Summit County Water Rescue; Purple Heart Alpacas; the scholarship recipient of the Adam Brown Award; and many others, too numerous to mention.

Leslie Christine Cook Dickerson

Health Care Studies Scholarship via Center Grove High School

Each year, a graduating senior from Center Grove High School is awarded a $1,000 scholarship. We award the scholarship on Senior Awards Day to a student who plans to pursue a health care studies program at a four-year college. We are part of the Center Grove Scholarship Foundation.

Jake and Travis Findley

Jake and Travis Arms of Life Fund

Jake and Travis lost their lives on February 3, 2007, when the SUV they were riding in collided with a train. The crossing did not have flashing lights or cross arms. The Jake and Travis Arms of Life Fund contributes to railroad-crossing upgrades, and helps implement railroad-crossing safety and education programs within our school systems. Please visit armsoflife.com for more information.

Nicolas William Habicht

IU Bloomington Scholarships via Center Grove High School

In remembrance of Nicolas Habicht, Joseph Alexander and Jake Surface, $1000 scholarships are presented each May to three seniors graduating from Center Grove High School who plan to attend IU Bloomington. Information is available through Center Grove High School's guidance office.

Friends Forever Memorial Golf Outing

In remembrance of Nicolas, Joseph, and Jake. A golf outing every August at Hickory Stick Golf Course in Greenwood, Indiana. Funds raised are used for scholarships; to purchase carbon monoxide detectors for individuals in need; and for donations to fire departments, food pantries, Christmas Angels and other needs that arise in the Center Grove area.

Abdul-Rahman Peter Kassig

Abdul-Rahman Peter Kassig Fund at SAMS

The Syrian American Medical Society, SAMS, runs hospitals and clinics providing the majority of medical care given to people engulfed in the Syrian conflict.

Syrian American Medical Society Foundation
3660 Stutz Dr., Suite 100
Canfield, Ohio 44406

Abdul-Rahman Peter Kassig Scholarship at Butler University

This scholarship supports an upper class student intent on pursuing humanitarian studies. For more information:
http://legacy.butler.edu/political-science/abdul-rahman-peter-kassig/

Jennifer Lynn Buxton Longworth & John "Dion" Longworth

Southwest Elementary Jennifer and Dion Longworth Memorial Award

Jennifer had a way of reaching students who were tough to reach. She loved "her kids." The Southwest Elementary PTO has created a special award to carry on her legacy of excellence in education with the hope that the recipients ofthis honor will carry on the love Jennifer had for learning as they further their education beyond high school. It is given to

264

a graduating Greenwood High School senior seeking continuing education. For the first ten years, it will be awarded to one of Jennifer Buxton Longworth's students. Thereafter, recipients will be selected based on the established criteria of excellence. Contributions to the fund can be made to the Johnson County Community Foundation *Longworth Fund* at JCCF, PO Box 217, Franklin, IN 46131.

Samuel Xavier Motsay

SAMs Watch

SAMs Watch shares the latest dangers of designer drugs to help explain the growing concerns of synthetic drugs across the nation. As young people and adults alike, educating ourselves is the best way we can combat this threat to our youth and better prepare parents and the communities we live in to deal with this threat, which is what we aim to do. For more information, please visit samswatch.org.

Peyton Ann Riekhof

The Peyton Riekhof Foundation for Youth Hope

A non-profit foundation which provides funding for suicide-prevention training and organizes community-wide mental health awareness programs. For more information, please visit www.thepeytonriekhoffoundation.com.

Play for Peyton Softball Tournament

A softball tournament, held each September in Fishers, Indiana, in memory of Peyton and her love of softball. Proceeds support the mental health awareness mission of The Peyton Riekhof Foundation for Youth Hope.

Patrick Andrew Trainor

Patrick A. Trainor Memorial Fund at Central Indiana Community Foundation

Established at Legacy Fund, an affiliate of Central Indiana Community Foundation, the Patrick A. Trainor Memorial Fund supports the Humane Society; Purdue University Pre-Vet Program; Cathedral High School; and Mothers Against Drunk Driving (MADD). For more information, please contact Philanthropic Services Advisor Becky Honeywell at BeckyH@CICF.org.

"Loss of a Child"

by Kelly Baltzell M.A. & Karen Baltzell Ph.D.*

1. **Crying is natural:** Cry as much and as often as you want and need. Let the tears flow either when you are alone or in public. Crying is a common outlet for grief. Do not apologize.

2. **Recognize that time does heal:** Your loss will be intense and long-lasting but it won't always knock you to your knees. Do not try to shortcut the grieving process.

3. **Beware of change:** Losing a child can feel like you have lost a physical part of yourself. The loss also puts into question your role as a parent. The loss of your child will change your world. Realize you still can make choices and have control over how you build your life after your loss.

4. **Feeling Guilty:** It is normal to feel guilt after the death of your child. You may feel guilty that you could have prevented his/her death. Also, you may feel guilty because you are unable to care or help your remaining children as much as you would like. If the guilt keeps getting worse, get professional help.

5. **Honor the life your child lived:** Do not try to hide it. Tell other people and family what a wonderful gift you had in your life. Sharing can help heal. Try to find meaning in your child's life.

6. **Watch for special dates:** Losing a child is losing the present and also the future. Special anniversary dates, holidays and birthdays can be doubly hard because not only are you grieving his/her loss, you are grieving the life your child would have had at that special time.

7. **Know gender differences:** Recognize that you and your spouse are most likely going to grieve differently. Try not to blame or criticize your spouse over his/her grieving. Your spouse is also the person who can support you the most. He or she have also lost their child. Lean on each other.

8. **Go to Therapy:** Losing a child is a pain that is indescribable. Do not try to manage this pain on your own. Seek out a grief therapist who can help monitor your mental health, help you make an action plan, and be there to listen when you need it the most.

9. **Watch for Depression:** Being sad and grieving is crippling. Being depressed is a chemical change in your brain. Depression is sometimes missed because it is thought to be "just grieving". If you think you are depressed get a doctor's evaluation. Do not disregard thoughts of suicide. If you are suicidal, call 911 or go to a hospital emergency room as soon as possible.

10. **Remember your remaining children and family:** Grieving affects all members of the family. Other children sometimes are forgotten or ignored by parents who are buried in their own grief. Find the energy to talk to your remaining children about their thoughts and feelings. Get a therapist for yourself and/or your other children if you do not have the strength to parent as well as grieve.

11. **Talk to family and friends:** Friends, family and those at work will not know how to help you or relate to you unless you are specific about your wants and needs. Tell others what you need so they do not fall short of your expectations. Ask for help - it is okay, and at this time in your life - essential.

12. **Lean on your faith:** Remember to touch base with your source of spirituality. It will bring comfort, strength and internal wisdom. If you have no belief system to help you through this rugged time, get in touch with nature. Perhaps this would be an appropriate time to reach out and explore new areas of thought. Or, seek out others who hurt in the same way.

"Helping Children Grieve"

by Kelly Baltzell M.A. & Karen Baltzell Ph.D.*

1. **Talk about the death:** Do not be afraid to talk about death with children. Kids are smart. They will realize things have changed. Be honest concerning your feelings with the children as well

2. **Model behavior of grief:** Children learn many things by mimicking behavior around them. Grieving in front of children will help them learn they can cry, laugh and be themselves when they are sad.

3. **Going to the final ceremony:** Explain what will happen at the ceremony. Answer children's questions the best you can - it will help their curiosity and their emotions.

4. **Realize the age and stage of death perception:** Grieving for children is different at each age-stage from infants onwards. Be aware of the age - stage and communicate with the child at that stage level. (see ages and stages pamphlet) .' .

5. **Talk to teachers in person:** Make an appointment to talk to a child's teacher directly about the death in the family. Set up a plan of action in case grades start to fail, if behavior starts to change and/or emotional outbreaks occur in the classroom.

6. **Provide an element of safety and reassurance;** Maintain routines as much as possible. Show affection and assurance that the child is loved and will not be abandoned. If the child has lost a parent, talk about who will be taking care of them and the family. A good way to reassure a child is through lots of touching.

7. **Let them feel:** Do not tell a child how they should or should not feel about the death. Children perceive death and accept it in different ways at different ages. Encourage them to talk and share their feelings. Accept them and their responses unconditionally. You need to be as stable as possible so that children can express a great range of emotion.

8. **Reassure children that they aren't going to die:** They did not cause the death and are not responsible for it by their behavior or thoughts. Emphasize to them that this particular death does not mean that they or someone else they love will die soon.

9. **Color and draw:** Give children an outlet to express their emotions. Drawing can help put emotions to paper. Make sure there are plenty of crayons, colored pencils and plain paper available at all times. Encourage them to draw. Have them make up stories about their picture. Do not censure or correct what they say, even though the facts may be incorrect.

10. **Read stories about death:** Buy a book that explains death to children. There are a few books such as "I had a friend named Peter" by Janice Cohn, D.5.W. Read the book with the child and answer any questions. Do not forget the public library. Check to find books to read to children about death and loss or ask the librarian to recommend books.

11. **See A Therapist:** Children are subject to depression just like adults. However, their symptoms can be different. Angry, mad, sad feelings are normal for them to feel. If a child's behavior changes radically be sure to take them to a therapist that specializes in dealing with children and grief. Do not wait to "see how it goes". Make an appointment right away.

12. **Use exact terms:** Use the words die and death. Do not use "passing", go to sleep, lost; tell exactly how it happened! 'The heart stopped beating" or the person had cancer of the liver. Otherwise children may think they caused the death or that a bad spirit did.

"Helping A Friend Through Grief"

by Kelly Baltzell M.A. & Karen Baltzell Ph.D.*

1. **Talk to your friend on an intimate level about their loss:** Talking about die death will probably be important to your friend. Do not be afraid to talk on a deep intimate level with your friend about the loss. Listen and be non-judgmental.

2. **Give options on how you can help:** People in grief cannot think clearly. Instead of asking how can I help you? Give specific items on how you can help. For example, "Can I mow the lawn? Do your laundry) Pick up people from the airport?"

3. **Make outreaches to your friend:** Grief can last up to three years after a death. Make an effort to reach out to your friend during this time. The grieving person does not always have the strength to reach out to others.

4. **Remember anniversaries:** After the funeral many people forget when a person died. Your friend will not have forgotten. Important dates to remember are the first, second, and third year after the death, birthdays, wedding anniversaries, holidays, the day the deceased became sick, and any other special day that was important to your friend and the deceased.

5. **Spend time with your friend:** Most likely, your friend will not call you. Grieving people often have little energy. Reaching out to make contact and saying, "Can you come over and be with me today?" is most likely difficult or impossible. Take the initiative to spend time with your friend.

6. **Know your friend is going to change:** Death and grief changes a person. Their world as they knew has been changed. Usually a death brings many other losses. Do not be angry or dismayed when see the changes happening.

7. **Watch for depression:** Grief and depression are not the same. Grief is normal. It happens after a death. Depression is a change in the chemical make-up of the brain. Warning signs your friend may be depressed are: sleeping all day, major weight gain or loss, lack of interest in activities that once were fun, and thoughts of suicide. Take all self-destructive conversations seriously. Call 911 or take your friend to the Emergency room.

8. **Be, an exercise buddy:** Offer to start working out with your friend. Exercise helps with grieving and sadness. Even going for a walk once a week may give you a great chance to spend some quality time with your friend and get some exercise at the same time.

9. **Do special things:** People tend to stop making contact with a grieving person a few weeks after the death. Do little special things for your friend. This could be from giving cards and flowers to offering to help weed the garden or cook a meal.

10. **Let them cry:** Crying is a natural part of grieving. Some people are uncomfortable and do not know what to do when a person is crying. Let them cry. Bring them some tissue and listen. Crying will make your friend feel better.

---

*The information on these three pages is from brochures obtained from Forrest Lawn Funeral Home and is reprinted here with permission of the authors.